ప్రియమైన వంశీ, ప్రకాశ్

శుభాకాంక్షలతో, ప్రేమతో

మీ

మఖీల్ రమేశు వడకలు

Leading with Aesthetics

Leading with Aesthetics

The Transformational Leadership of Charles M. Vest at MIT

Mahesh Daas

LEXINGTON BOOKS
Lanham • Boulder • New York • London

Published by Lexington Books
An imprint of The Rowman & Littlefield Publishing Group, Inc.
4501 Forbes Boulevard, Suite 200, Lanham, Maryland 20706
www.rowman.com

Unit A, Whitacre Mews, 26-34 Stannary Street, London SE11 4AB

British Library Cataloguing in Publication Information Available

Library of Congress Cataloging-in-Publication Data

Daas, Mahesh.
Leading with aesthetics : the transformational leadership of Charles M. Vest at MIT / Mahesh Daas.
pages cm.
Includes bibliographical references and index.
ISBN 978-1-4985-0249-8 (cloth : alk. paper) -- ISBN 978-1-4985-0250-4 (electronic)
1. Vest, Charles M. 2. Educational leadership--Massachusetts--Cambridge. 3. Massachusetts Institute
of Technology--Presidents I. Title
T171.M49D33 2015
658.4'09201--dc23
                    2015015514

Printed in the United States of America

To my mother and the loving memory of my late father whose unconditional love, dutifulness, hard work, dedication to family, belief in education, tons of patience, and wisdom helped raise our family from modest beginnings to prosperity.

Contents

List of Figures

List of Tables

Foreword

For as long as organizations have existed, so have leaders. They are held in high esteem, when things go right, that is. And they quickly become targets when things go wrong. This book focuses on those aspects that went right at the Massachusetts Institute of Technology (MIT). Yet, from the middle of the transformation described here, tensions existed between two interpretations: a belief that the investments in the institution were positive, and a belief they were not. Furthermore, these tensions were not simply about the buildings or the choice of architects but about what MIT was and what it wanted to become. The tensions were as emotional as they were logical. Anyone who has been part of contentious situations knows what that tension feels like. Perhaps you have experienced the joys and pleasures of a positive reconciliation and of beneficial conclusions. You may also have felt the downs associated with negative outcomes. It is the feeling, sensing aspect of organizational leadership that is the focus of this book.

In addition to presenting the story of how one president transformed a physical campus from one thing into another, it is about the ways in which humans interact with each other, experience the world and the organizations they inhabit, and understand. Too often leadership studies are operational; they miss the tacit connections that must exist and the ways in which people connect to each other and to their surroundings. This study impressively looks at leadership as a human endeavor, and it does so through a novel lens. At its core is the role of the leader in the heart, mind, and soul of the institution and with those individuals who comprise its community. Leadership is as much about feeling and sensing as it is about doing or thinking. In many ways leadership is a felt experience. It is that something that we sense that moves us collectively forward. Of course, it also can include repulsion; ask anyone who has worked for an ineffective or unethical leader.

This study helps readers understand how concepts not typically associated with leadership—such as beauty, sublimity, and delight—can matter. It helps put the person and her or his senses back into the human dynamic that is leadership. Leadership is about human connections. As this case study demonstrates, these ties are sometimes interpersonal ones close at hand, but other times they are through a distance and with mediators, physical as is the case in this book and otherwise, between the leader and the led.

Colleges and universities seek leaders capable of addressing the litany of challenges they face, such as increasing the participation rates of those historically under-served; improving the graduation and completion rates for all who enter; tamping down the continued escalation of costs; ensuring learning so that students, families, and employers are confident graduates know what colleges and universities purport they have learned; and providing breakthrough thought and knowledge to address the city's, region's, state's, and the nation's, if not the world's, most pressing problems. At the same time, it seems like solutions abound from elected officials, influential private foundations, media pundits, think tanks, and academics to name a few who willingly share their opinions on what to do. Advice simply pursued and implemented can and should address the shortcomings, they argue or hope. What is missing from these discussions is the catalyst that can ensure the solutions to today's problems are effective: leadership. The conversation about higher education's problems can and should include a focused discussion of the needed leadership to address these challenges and many others brushed over in the list above. Without leadership, good ideas are not implemented and the status quo remains deeply embedded. This book helps turn that tide.

Finally, what is missing too much from talk and reflections about higher education and its challenges are the values and purpose of the enterprise, another key aspect of the human dimensions central to this book. Budgets, outcomes, efficiencies and the like matter, but values and purposes are important in higher education as well. Too many discussions focus on the former and not enough on the latter. Values and purposes are the avenues through which institutions and their leaders connect to the people and communities they serve. Innovation, boldness, and cutting-edge practices are defining and constantly present values in this study. A focus on aesthetics reminds us of values and meaning and how they should matter and need to be made an explicit part of intentional, ongoing institutional dialogue and debate.

In sum, this is a book that looks at parts of organizations and leadership too often out of the spotlight. As theorist James March reminds students of organization in his essay "Footnotes to Organizational Change," "Organizations need to maintain a balance . . . between explicitly sensible processes of change (problem-solving, learning, planning) and certain elements of foolishness. . . ." (March, 1981, p. 572). It is difficult to alter the balance between those elements, which is exactly what Charles Vest did at MIT. Through design, and by extension aesthetics, Vest elevated the essential foolishness needed to transform MIT. As March writes, "The mix of organizational foolishness and rationality is deeply embedded in the rules, incentives, and beliefs of the society and organization. It is possible to imagine changing the mix of rules, thereby changing the level of foolishness; but it is hard to imagine being able to modify broad cultural and organizational attributes with much precision or control." (p. 574). Vest accomplished that difficult task, as you'll soon read.

This book raises meaningful questions, provides an underappreciated lens through which to view decisions, and tells a wonderful story of institutional transformation. It provides an interesting and meaningful way to understand the impact Vest had on MIT over his fourteen years, but it does much more. It reminds us of the importance of sense, feeling, and understanding in academic leadership, of how and why people connect, and of the significance of those connections to advancing an enterprise about which many care deeply.

Peter Eckel
Senior Fellow and Director of Leadership Programs
University of Pennsylvania

Preface

This is a book that stands at the intersections between disciplines. Aesthetics, architecture, leadership studies, psychoanalysis, and organizational behavior are an eclectic array of fields from which this book draws. It is a risky proposition, even a fool's errand, to embark on a scholarly journey that claims to shed new light on our understanding of organizational leadership. As someone trained in architecture and urban design, it was almost natural for me to look at the questions of leadership through lenses of design. Despite the oceans of ink spilled over the topic of leadership, I felt there was something missing from the scholarly and popular discourses that mostly exist in disciplinary silos. I had a hunch that my education in architecture, urban design, business management, and higher education management would help me prepare an alchemical mix of off-the-scholarly-shelf elements that would result in a unique leadership potion. But, before I could get too excited about my hunch, I needed to find real stories that would reveal elements that were suitable for the study. I found them in the story of President Charles M. Vest and his leadership team at the Massachusetts Institute of Technology.

In fact, the seeds for this book were sown long before I even knew that I would be writing this book. The late William Mitchell, who served as the dean of MIT's School of Architecture and Planning, was a longtime mentor for me. As far back as 2001, whenever we met, he spoke enthusiastically about the story of organizational and architectural transformations occurring at MIT. I particularly cherish the personal tour of the MIT campus he gave me in 2008 that left an indelible impression on me. After his untimely death in 2010, and during my time at the University of Pennsylvania's executive doctorate program where significant research for this book took place, things began to fall in place serendipitously.

When I began looking to cases of academic presidential leadership where significant and intentional organizational change was brought about that involved large-scale architectural transformations, I thought I would have difficulty choosing from many stories. As I looked at case after case, I realized how rarely the physical transformation of an academic institution comes about as a result of deliberate intentionality and informed vision of a president. As I explain at the end of the book, only one case rose to the top to meet the criteria I set forth for my study.

Since I started writing the book, I have spoken to scores of university presidents and discussed the book's subject matter with them. In every case, I received tremendous interest and genuine curiosity to understand how the frameworks of aesthetics could empower organizational leadership. I hope my book provides enough insight for scholars and leaders alike to expand and deepen the research and practice of leadership.

Mahesh Daas
Association of Collegiate Schools of Architecture Distinguished Professor

Acknowledgments

This book could not have been written without the generosity of late MIT President **Charles M. Vest**. True to his reputation he was forthright, insightful, open, and held nothing back. He agreed to meet with me despite his quickly deteriorating health at that time. I owe him my heartfelt gratitude for sharing his story.

I am deeply thankful for nearly two decades of mentorship by **William J. Mitchell**, the late dean of MIT's School of Architecture and Planning. This book is a tribute to his courage, unbridled enthusiasm for architectural innovation, and his significant partnership with President Vest that transformed MIT.

I would like to acknowledge the unfettered access granted by my interviewees, who were part of Vest's leadership team at various points of his presidency. These men and women were immensely generous with their time and insights that helped me piece together a complex and multifaceted story: President **Robert Brown** of Boston University who served as provost of MIT; **Lawrence Bacow**, member of Harvard Corporation and president emeritus of Tufts University who served as chancellor of MIT under President Vest; **John Curry** of Huron Associates, who served as executive vice president of MIT; **Ray Stata**, who is a trustee of MIT and cofounder and chairman of the board of Analog Devices, Inc.; **Christopher Terman** of MIT's Computer Science and Artificial Intelligence Laboratory; **Victoria Sirianni**, who served as the director of MIT's facilities; **Robert Simha**, who served as MIT's director of planning office; and **Stephen Immerman**, president of Montserrat College of Art, who served as executive director of enterprise services and associate dean for student life at MIT.

The roots of this book go back to the dissertation research I conducted at the University of Pennsylvania as part of my studies in the executive doctorate program in higher education management. **Peter Eckel**, senior fellow and director of leadership programs at the University of Pennsylvania's Alliance for Higher Education and Democracy served as the dissertation advisor and has kindly written the foreword for this book. I am deeply thankful for his erudition and consistent guidance which have played a major role in advancing the research that eventually led to this book. **Matthew Hartley**, the head of higher education division at the University of Pennsylvania's Graduate School of Education and **Phil Schubert**, president of Abilene Christian University, served on the committee and provided valuable insights throughout the research and writing process. The committee's constant encouragement and recognition of the value of leading with aesthetics have helped evolve my research into this book.

All of my classmates and staff at the executive doctorate program at Penn have become an extended family: **Mercedes Ramirez Bartolomei**, assistant chancellor and assistant provost for student diversity at the University of Illinois at Urbana-Champaign; **Xavier Cole**, vice president for student affairs at Washington College; **Melanie Corn**, provost of California College of Arts; **Noemi Crespo**, chief student affairs officer at Johns Hopkins University School of Advanced International Studies; **Gretchen Dobson**, global alumni relations consultant, Gretchen Dobson LLC; **Stacia Edwards**, associate vice president of academic affairs and special assistant to the president at Columbus State Community College; **Allan Gozum**, vice president for finance at Benedictine University; **Jose Guzman**, president of Universidad de los Andes, Chile; **Jim Lai**, faculty of dentistry at the University of Toronto; **Linda Luciano**, trustee of Caldwell University; **Kiernan Mathews**, director of COACHE Project at Harvard Graduate School of Education; **Amy McCormack**, senior vice president for finance and administration at Dominican University; **Peggy McCready**, director of academic technology services at New York University; **Betsy Newman**, vice president of student affairs and dean of students at Berklee College of Music; **Philip Rogers**, vice president and chief of staff at American Council on Education; **Sean Ryan**, vice president for enrollment management at Bellarmine University; **Richard (Sal) Salcido**, The William Redman Professor of Physical Medicine & Rehabilitation, senior fellow, Institute on Aging, associate, Institute for Medical Bioengineering at the University of Pennsylvania; **Aslan Sarinzhipov**, minister of education and science, Kazakhstan; **Candace Thille**, assistant professor at the Graduate School of Education at Stanford University; **Melissa Trotta**, vice president of Brill Neumann Associates; **Hoopes Wampler**, assistant vice president of alumni relations at the University of Pennsylvania; **Wayne Williams**, chair of department of business administration, Community College of Philadelphia; **Becky Wyke**, vice chancellor for finance and administration at The University of Maine system; and **Ginger O'Neil**, program coordinator, executive doctorate in higher education management at the University of Pennsylvania. Together we have become each other's strength. Their wholehearted support, constructive feedback, and encouragement to write this book served as wind in my sails! I am deeply thankful for their friendship.

Marybeth Gasman, professor at the Graduate School of Education at the University of Pennsylvania and **Douglas E. Clark**, vice president of enrollment management at Ferrum College, were instrumental in sharing their wisdom, strongly encouraging me to write this book, reading my book proposal, and guiding me through the book writing process.

I also wish to acknowledge the early guidance provided by Professor **Michael Useem**, William and Jacalyn Egan Professor of Management and director of the Center for Leadership and Change Management at the Wharton School, University of Pennsylvania.

I sincerely acknowledge the steadfast support of Dean **Guillermo Vásquez de Velasco** of Ball State University's College of Architecture and Planning throughout the research and writing process.

Part of the research for this book was made possible through the generous support of the **Irving Distinguished Professorship** of the College of Architecture and Planning at Ball State University. I am deeply grateful to the Irving family endowment fund for their kind support.

Barbara White Bryson, vice president for strategic planning and analysis at The University of Arizona, and a fellow graduate of the executive doctorate program at Penn, was very helpful in making key connections at the MIT facilities department, and provided constant encouragement. **Pamela Delphenich**, former director of campus planning at MIT, was very generous with her time, advice, and a comparative assessment of the campus planning processes at MIT and Yale University. **William L. Porter**, former dean of the School of Architecture and Planning at MIT, graciously shared his thoughts about the role of the school's deans in shaping the MIT campus.

I wish to thank **James Langley** of Langley Innovations for closely reading an early draft and providing constructive criticism to significantly refine this book.

I wish to gratefully acknowledge the rigorous eye and impeccable responsiveness of my copy editor **Christine Rhine**.

I thank **Lynne Damianos**, who enthusiastically leaped at the opportunity to partner with me to provide masterful photographs of the MIT campus, which richly illustrate this book and its cover.

Lastly, but most importantly, my wife **Madhavi**, daughter **Charmi**, and son **Chirag** have been enormously understanding of me. My mother **Jhansi** and sister **Veni** have been sources of immeasurable spiritual strength that I have constantly relied on through the thick and thin of my journey. I certainly wish my late father **Kabir** was here to rejoice in the release of this book, but I do feel his blessings every moment. My family's unwavering support and boundless patience have laid a strong foundation that underlies my scholarly endeavors and professional advancements.

Introduction

Leadership is the primary subject matter of this book. In these pages, I examine the aesthetic dimension of transformational leadership through an eclectic blend of lenses primarily drawn from the fields of architecture, political science, organizational aesthetics, and organizational psychoanalysis. A detailed case study of the leadership of Charles Marstiller Vest (1941–2013), who served as the president of Massachusetts Institute of Technology for fourteen years between 1990 and 2004 will illustrate the importance of the aesthetic dimension in leadership and organizational change.

This book examines the role of aesthetics in organizational transformation and leadership, particularly in the context of academic institutions. Leadership has been thus far predominantly examined from the perspective of function (performance) and position in the organizational structure (such as a CEO or a president). Relatively little work has been done in studying leadership of academic institutions, let alone from the perspective of aesthetics, which this book aims to rectify. Although aesthetic dimension is important in any organizational context, it is particularly important for academic institutions of all kinds.

Although the primary audience for this book is scholars and practitioners of leadership, I hope the study will also inform leaders at all levels in the academic world and leaders in other organizational sectors. Scholars of leadership in different fields, including education, business, political science, psychology, and social sciences, will find the research to be relevant.

Architects working in the educational sector and those working for institutions will be interested in understanding the leadership perspective, power dynamics, aesthetic possibilities, and institutional processes explored in this study. Architects will also be interested in understanding how frameworks of architecture and design can be applied to areas other than architecture, such as in leadership, organizational behavior, and strategic decision making.

Trustees will be interested in understanding the importance of choosing aesthetic and transformational leaders with moral fiber. They will also be able to frame architecture in a new way—far from the conventional real estate development frame or stylistic frames that are all too common on many campuses.

Treasurers and vice presidents in all areas of the higher education sector will be interested in knowing their roles and limitations when it comes to the matters of architecture and how financial resources should serve, not dictate, institutional mission.

Anyone even remotely connected to MIT will be interested in learning, for the first time, the comprehensive story of how an aesthetic leader transformed a rundown gray factory "in bed with the feds" into a top university in the world with a campus that is in line with its transformed identity as a diversified institution that innovates and takes risks.

Aesthetics and Organizations

If you are reading this book, it is likely you have walked across a stage wearing ceremonial robes and shaken a hand or two on the way to grabbing a symbolic diploma from a dean or a president dressed in more colorful and flowingly oversized regalia. In the background, you likely heard the familiar "Pomp and Circumstance" floating over the buzz of the festive crowd of family and friends. It must have been a remarkable experience, a memorable one. Needless to say, I am referring to a graduation ceremony at an academic institution, an occasion full of colors, order, form, textures, smells, sounds, and perhaps the taste of champagne. Aesthetic experiences punctuate key moments in institutional life. Without such experiences, life and organizations would be, well, not as meaningful or memorable. The more foundational an organization is in society, the more aesthetic it is. Academic institutions, military, religious organizations, and courts of justice are institutions replete with aesthetic experiences, formality, and symbolism.

Aesthetics is commonly characterized as a philosophical study of beauty; although this is true to some extent and in some circumstances, I use the word to mean something more. Aesthetics is often misunderstood as an extraneous, superficial, *post facto* addition to a thing or experience. As I will explain in the book, aesthetics is foundational to our experience as human beings and essential to how we encounter the world in a way that defines our identity and affirms our existence. Life without aesthetic experiences is a life without significance. An institution devoid of aesthetic dimension is an institution without significance or consequence.

Aesthetics has been a topic of much philosophical and political discourse since antiquity. A long lineage of thinkers in the East and the West have written tomes on the topic of aesthetics. Aesthetic experiences are sensory experiences that awaken the five senses and heighten the feeling of being alive. The sense of being alive is a bodily feeling. I take a more pragmatic view of the topic and operationalize aesthetics in this book by contrasting it with its opposite, anesthetics, numbing the senses and feelings.

Aesthetics is the study of tacit and explicit knowledge (Polanyi, 1967) gained through *sensory experiences* and the resulting visceral *feelings* (Gagliardi, 1990; Strati, 2010). Sight, sound, touch, taste, and smell are the five routes through which we physically experience and internalize the world. Experience precedes thought. Of the thousands of sensations we encounter every day, a few stand out for their intensity, engagement, and distinctiveness. Aesthetic experiences are experiences that activate the senses and leave palpable and visceral feelings and emotions. Experiences that in particular encompass more than one sense, such as erotic experiences, are some of the most powerful moments in life.

In Western Greenlandic language, there are eighteen different words and thirty-two more variants to describe snow and ice (Bittner, 1986; Fortescue, 1984). In the same vein, there are multiple words that describe different aesthetic experiences. Although often aesthetics is equated with *beauty*, words such as sublime, tragic, comic, holy, picturesque, gracious, and grotesque could also be classified as aesthetic experiences that often go misunderstood. Beauty elicits attraction and positive pleasure; sublimity elicits awe and humility; grotesqueness repulses and disgusts; tragedy elicits pain and grief; and comedy evokes hilarity and buoyancy (Strati, 2010).

Aesthetics and symbols differ from each other in that aesthetics is about how the world *presents* itself to the senses as phenomena, and symbols are about *representing* a reality or an abstract concept not otherwise presentable to the senses. Aesthetics and symbols are not unrelated. Symbols have their aesthetics. In the context of the present study, aesthetic experiences presented by architecture have been chosen for focused consideration for aforementioned reasons.

The pervasiveness of aesthetics and our desire to seek out aesthetic experiences—through music or film or adventure sports or any number of other experiences—might make it difficult for us to truly understand how foundational aesthetics are to being human. The power and prevalence of aesthetics are easily underestimated by the sheer fact that every moment of life we yearn for such experiences. Life is animated by aesthetic experiences of varying intensities. Meaningful existence is defined by powerful aesthetic experiences that punctuate one's life. Who in his sane mind seeks out bland, insipid, boring, and numbing experiences except those inundated by pain and sensory overload? The notions of sensibility, senselessness, making sense, and sensitivity are all aesthetic notions implicating our sensory experiences. The widespread usage of these terms suggests how deeply ingrained aesthetics are in our lives.

Leadership in Academic Institutions

In recent times, American colleges and universities have been under attack from all quarters of society for failings in a range of areas including

mission-critical ones of access, affordability, accountability, and scalabil-
ity (Arum & Roksa, 2010; Bok, 2006; Massy, 2003; Zemsky, 2009; Zemsky
& Finney, 2010; Zumeta, Callan, Breneman, & Finney, 2011). There is a
menacing sense that the world of higher education is adrift without effective leaders, raising the question "who is in charge?" Some scholars answer that "nobody is in charge" (Lazerson, 2010); others say leadership
doesn't matter very much (Cohen & March 1986; Birnbaum, 1992), suggesting that either there is a lack of leadership (talent or training problem) or the scope of leadership and its effectiveness are intrinsically limited by the form and structure of higher education institutions (organizational design problem). Examples, however, do exist of leaders who have
brought about important and meaningful changes that challenge these
assumptions. The book studies a particular instance in which leadership
mattered and made a difference.

Psychodynamics of Transformational Leadership

In a classic work that analyzed political leaders such as Mahatma
Gandhi and Abraham Lincoln, James MacGregor Burns defined *transforming leadership* as that relationship between a leader and followers that
transcends the routine transactions of an organization and helps each
achieve greater levels of self-actualization (Burns, 1978a). Transforming
leadership occurs, he said, "when one or more persons *engage* with others
in such a way that leaders and followers raise one another to higher
levels of motivation and morality" (Burns, 1978, p. 20).

Burns described transformational leadership as fundamentally *moral*
leadership. He explored and employed a transformational leadership
framework using Freudian and Jungian psychoanalytical frameworks as
he focused more on motivation and development rather than behavior.
Burns warned that transformational leaders are not to be mistaken for
dictatorial, authoritarian, self-aggrandizing, and egocentric personalities.
He observed that one sign of transforming leadership is that the followers (or team members) become transforming leaders themselves and actualize their full potential in the process. Burns concluded that transforming "leaders help transform followers' needs into positive *hopes* and *aspirations*" (ibid.). Thus, engagement transcends the immediate task or project goals and addresses the higher needs of the individual, and through
the mutual engagement, the follower is elevated to a higher level of morality and self-actualization.

Most scholarship on university presidential leadership addresses the
category of what Burns called transactional leadership (Birnbaum, 1992).
Relatively little writing exists about transformational presidential leadership in the higher education sector (Fisher, 1984; Fisher, Tack, & Wheeler,
1988; Fisher & Koch, 1996b; Kerr, 1984; Kerr, 2001). Transformational
leadership appears to be rare—but not impossible and certainly not un-

desirable—in academic institutions. Few books exploring the efficacy of transformational leadership in universities have found encouraging results (Grafton, 2009; Grosso, 2008; Head, 2009; Hempowicz, 2010). In a limited study at a private, religiously affiliated doctoral research university, Grosso (2008) found that faculty put in extra effort and expressed higher job satisfaction if they perceived the president to be transformational. Grosso's study also showed that in such instances of transformational presidential leadership, faculty exhibited the morale and motivation to transcend self-interest for the benefit of the institutional goals. Head (2009) in a study of three faith-based liberal arts colleges found that transformational leadership played a key role in the turnaround of the institutions and that all three presidents' use of symbolic leadership was an essential part of their leadership approach. Hempowicz (2010) found that the vitality of U.S. Department of Education Title III and Title V-eligible private colleges (federally categorized—either by mission or by enrolled student population—as institutions supporting specific minority populations such as Native American, Black, Hispanic, etc.) was dependent on the transformational characteristics of the institutions' presidents.

Of the different institutional transformations that could be addressed in the context of higher education—such as curricula, research policies, athletics, advancement, student life, tenure, diversity, and other issues—the current study focuses on a specific topic of how leadership impacts and is impacted by the transformation of organizational aesthetics of the physical plant (campus) of a higher education institution. Approaching leadership from the organizational aesthetics perspective is significant for two reasons. Leadership, as an organizational phenomenon, is centrally implicated in the management and orchestration of organizational aesthetics. Bolman and Deal's (2008) four frames briefly described aesthetics under the symbolic frame but did not offer a substantive discussion or distinction between aesthetic and symbolic frames or between experiential and cognitive frames.

The emphasis on architecture is both unique and important because architecture is the most concrete, enduring, and permanent embodiment of institutional mission (Bergquist & Pawlak, 2008) and provides an existential foothold for its constituents (Norberg-Schulz, 1980). Architecture is also the most challenging and strategic form of change due to the amount of resources needed, the number of constituents involved, and the time it takes to conceptualize, plan, and construct, and the lifespan—sometimes thousands of years—once a structure is built. The architecture of an organization is a fundamental organizational artifact that provides the most tangible, spatial, and material continuity for an organization's mission, identity, and meaning (Broadbent, Bunt, & Jencks, 1980; Eco, 1979; Giedion, 1967; Jencks, 1991; Preziosi, 1979; Rykwert, 1982; Strati, 1999c; Strati, 2010). Architectural transformations epitomize deep organizational and leadership processes that involve not just functional and financial decision making, but also aesthetic choices that craft organizational experiences. The aesthetic dimension of architecture is of particular importance to the current study.

The Exemplar Case of Presidential Leadership at MIT

Charles Marstiller Vest's fourteen-year-long presidency at MIT has been chosen as a single-site, *exemplar*[1] case study to explore the broad themes of transformational leadership and aesthetic transformations (see Appendix B: Research Design and Methods for more about site selection).

The case is significant for many reasons. MIT has been an exceptionally important institution in the United States and the world, particularly since the First and Second world wars. The current study examines a specific slice of Vest's presidency explored through the lens of organizational aesthetics. Vest's presidency started at the end of the Cold War that marked the decline of public support for research universities and the beginning of the World Wide Web. The phenomenal changes in the world provide a tumultuous and exciting backdrop for Vest's presidency.

By the time he stepped down from the presidency in 2004, Vest was the second longest serving president in MIT's history. Under his tenure, a number of consequential issues were tackled including advocacy for science and technology education in the United States, reforming student life at MIT, launching of OpenCourseWare, enhancing gender diversification at MIT, standing up to the lawsuit by the U.S. Department of Justice against Ivy League and other elite universities, and reforming and transforming the MIT campus at a scale unprecedented since the Cambridge campus opened in 1916 (Vest, 2005).

Vest's case has much to offer to presidents and other academic leaders, particularly within the context of the basic assumptions about the inevitability and prevalence of transactional leadership in academic institutions across the higher education sector.

William Mitchell, late dean of the MIT School of Architecture and architectural advisor to Vest, proclaimed, "MIT, under President Charles Vest, was rebuilt as radically as Rome under Septimus Severus" (Mitchell, 2007). Although the architectural transformations during Vest's presidency had been reported from an architectural perspective (Gannon, 2004; Hughes, 2008; Joyce & Gehry, 2004; Mitchell, 2007), no detailed account of his leadership of architectural transformation or about the other accomplishments exists. Some of the protagonists of Vest's plans had described the campus transformations as "the battle for the soul of MIT," which clearly points to underlying issues concerning organizational identity and the resistance to change (Mitchell, 2007). Vest has been credited with leading a billion-dollar campus transformation that added five major works of architecture and landscape architecture (designed, in partnership with local architectural firms, by prominent architects Charles Correa, Steven Holl, Frank Gehry, Fumihiko Maki, and Kevin Roche, and landscape architect Laurie Olin). More than 1.5 million square feet of space, which is a quarter of the campus, was added in a decade (Mitchell, 2007). The architectural merits, project costs, choice of star architects, and the neglect of existing buildings had all been topics of caustic debate since the plan was introduced. However, the facts remain that a tremendous amount of resources was committed and new building space was created to address pent-up demand, and the campus gained new icons that changed not just the experiences of campus but shifted the center of the campus from the Greek Classical complex on the Charles River to the northeast side of campus now dominated by the Ray and Maria Stata Center designed by Frank Gehry. Change happened, and it has generated as much praise as consternation from different constituents (Mitchell, 2007; Vest, 2005), confirming the transformative nature of the change (Levy & Merry, 1986; Van de Ven & Poole, 1995).

Aesthetics, Architecture, and Institutions

Why are the lenses of aesthetics and architecture important for academic presidential leadership? What relevance does this study have for higher education leadership today?

An institution without its architecture is like a soul without a body or a person without a face. Architecture is the index of an institution. Like faces and indices, architecture gives concrete presence, tangible ambiance, and definitive experiences for the otherwise abstract organizations that we call institutions. Institutions—more than any other type of organizations—depend on architecture to deliver on their missions for the primary reason that they are the foundations upon which the society stands and looks to as existential anchors. Institutions can survive for centuries, and architecture becomes the vehicle for institutions to provide continuity and solidity. Great institutions such as Harvard University, Cambridge University, Oxford University, and the University of Pennsylvania have thrived for many centuries and continue to do so as unique places. Most foundational institutions such as the Supreme *Court,* White *House,* city *hall* of any major city, Senate *Chamber,* and Carnegie *Foundation* and are identified by architecture contained in their name and are defined by specific architectural spaces that formalize the institutional configurations.

Decisions about architecture, as the study shows, reveal a leader's ability to translate mission into the most enduring forms of an institution. Architectural decisions also reveal an institution's inner struggles, conflicts, fears, aspirations, underlying values, and competing identities over long periods of time. Also, as the most experiential form of *tacit knowledge* that an institution can ever create, architecture becomes the most tangible facet of an institution and its mission of knowledge creation. Architecture is a womb in which great ideas are conceived, strategies are hatched, learning is facilitated, memories are created, and institutional mission is delivered.

Architecture is at once the most ubiquitous and yet least understood form of knowledge, a place that engenders familiarity but not necessarily understanding of its spaces and structure. Architecture is usually the most expensive asset of an institution. For instance, Harvard University's real estate assets are its single largest investment at $10.2 billion compared to the next biggest private equity investment at $7 billion (Harvard University, 2012). MIT's real estate and assets are valued at $2.5 billion as the single-largest investment for the institute (MIT Treasurer's Report, 2012).

The Presidential Vantage Point

The president of an institution, who enjoys the highest vantage point in the institution, has the deepest view of the institution and has the potential to understand the most about the unconscious life of the institution. The president carries the responsibility of ensuring the most faithful expression of the mission through the physical plant and its aesthetics that go beyond mere style and optics. No other individual in an institution can possibly have the same privileged and nearly all-pervasive view of the innards of an institution. Trustees, vice presidents, deans, directors of facilities, faculty, and architects who are hired for a job cannot play the central role that a president can play.

To that end, this book presents an in-depth account of a president's journey into architecture, a journey that transformed him and his institution in ways neither had expected. In the due course of the story, Vest is examined in situations that called for leadership amid difficult and challenging yet inspiring circumstances.

This book is organized into two distinct parts and a total of seven chapters. The first chapter presents a survey of theories of leadership in order to provide a larger context for how our understanding of leadership has evolved with the times. An understanding of the current context of leadership research is important to fully comprehend the importance of leading with aesthetics.

The second chapter examines transformational leadership theories with a focus on James MacGregor Burns's forty-year-old framework. Aesthetic leadership frameworks build on transformational leadership frameworks. The chapter also traces similar notions proposed by Abraham Zaleznik around the same time as Burns. Coincidentally or otherwise, both Burns and Zaleznik based their theories on psychoanalysis, to which the chapter pays particular attention. Filling a void in our understanding of transformational leadership in academic institutions, this chapter also addresses the role and relevance of transformational leadership in academic institutions.

The third and fourth chapters are the heart of this book. These chapters propose aesthetic approaches to deepen our understanding of organizations and leadership. Building on literature from many fields of study, these chapters advance a coherent framework for aesthetic leadership.

The fifth chapter then wraps up the discourse about aesthetic leadership by engaging the notion of organizational identity and cultures, particularly in the context of academic institutions.

Part 2 largely deals with an in-depth and illustrative case study of the presidential leadership of Charles Marstiller Vest, who served as the president of MIT.

The sixth chapter narrates the story of Vest's leadership in transforming MIT by taking an aesthetic approach to organizational change. This chapter has been written in a way to stand by itself.

The seventh chapter is where the two parts of the book come together through a detailed analysis of Vest's leadership case through the lenses of transformational leadership and organizational aesthetics.

NOTES

1. An exemplar has been defined by Thomas Kuhn (Kuhn, 1970; Nickles, 2002) as one of the components that go into the making of a paradigm and act as an essential foundation upon which the rest of the knowledge is built. An exemplar case becomes an essential study that cannot be satisfactorily explained using previous paradigms, challenges previous paradigms, and contributes to the construction of a new paradigm.

I

ONE

Leadership

What is Leadership?

In an orchestral performance consisting of dozens of accomplished musicians, there is one individual, the conductor, who plays no instrument. The conductor delicately holds a slender baton and stands in front of the orchestra. What is the role of the conductor? What is his relevance? The music is written on sheets, and the musicians are world class, so surely they can perform without him. They could, of course, but you might not want to hear the results. The conductor is the key to the interpretation of the piece, its tempo, the cueing, and the unifying of the orchestra both on and off the stage. Like conductors, good leaders create environments, unify purposes, and bring meaning to institutions (Talgam, 10/2009).

"Leadership is one of the most observed and least understood phenomena on earth," said the legendary political scientist, historian, and Pulitzer Prize winner James MacGregor Burns (1978). Thousands of books and articles have been written and are being written every day about the phenomenon of leadership. There have been as many definitions of leadership as there have been writings about it. Scholars and leaders from vastly different disciplines have framed, approached, conceptualized, and defined leadership from vastly different perspectives. However, the notions and frameworks of leadership have evolved (and will continue to evolve) over time, and have gained momentum with the advent of scientific research (Day & Antonakis, 2011). Leadership is not a phenomenon that can be defined once and for all; rather, the understanding, role, and interpretation of leadership will evolve with the social, cultural, and political context of the day. The research about leadership will need to take into account the inherent ambiguities and social-cultural factors in reinterpreting leadership.

The Landscape of Leadership Research

Day and Antonakis (2011) classify leadership research into nine categories: trait theories (1900s to present), behavioral theories (1930s–1970s), contingency theories (1930s–late 2000s), contextual or situational theories (1960s–2000s), skeptics of leadership (1970s), relational theories (1970s–present), new leadership (transformational) theories (1970s–present), information processing theories (1980s–present), and biological/evolutionary theories (since 2010s). Bernard Bass's magnum opus *Handbook of Leadership* has provided the most comprehensive summaries, classification systems, and taxonomies of leadership theories, practices, and applications (Bass, 1985b; Bass, Stogdill, & Stogdill, 1990). Also worth mentioning are the summative works of Gary Yukl (2011), Nitin Nohria, and Rakesh Khurana, who provided a multi-disciplinary perspective of the current state of scholarly inquiry about leadership (Nohria & Khurana, 2010).

The **trait approaches** spring from the platform that leaders are distinguishable from non-leaders by a set of special personality attributes or traits that make them leaders. Early theories and research tried to find correlations between leadership success and certain mystical qualities of leaders such as the abilities to intuit, persuade, and envision (Yukl, 2011). Psychodynamic approaches partially fall under the trait school and aim to explore the subconscious or unconscious motivations and drives that contribute to a leader's effectiveness (Day & Antonakis, 2011). Trait theories exclusively focus on leaders, not on the followers or the context. The simplicity and elegance, as well as over a hundred years of research, make the trait approaches the most examined ones in leadership research (Northouse, 2013).

The **behavioral approaches** focus on observable behaviors of leaders and managers. These approaches look for what leaders do, how they structure their work, and what they employ to resolve conflicts and overcome constraints to accomplish their goals. Some meta-research dubbed behavioral approaches as "style approaches" (ibid.). Behavioral approaches are distinguishable from trait approaches in that they shift the focus from the constitution of the leaders to the manifest actions of leaders, or what they actually do. The limitation of behavioral approaches appear to be their failure to show any definitive link between leadership behavior and universal effectiveness (ibid.).

Situational or contextual approaches focus on the context and the situational factors that influence the process of leadership. Situational approaches examine the organizational context, levels, and hierarchies and look for differences in the nature and differences between the leadership processes at different levels of organization (Yukl, 2011). Situational theories account for 80 percent of all leadership training programs in the Fortune 500 companies (Northouse, 2013). One of the strengths of this approach is its applicability for leadership practitioners and its focus on practice. This approach also suggests leaders need to adapt different styles at different levels of an organization and put into practice different skills depending on the context.

Contingency approaches are a subset of contextual approaches. Contingency theories are concerned with matching leadership style with specific situations. Hence, these theories are also called "leader-match" theories. Contingency theory researchers make empirically grounded predictions and generalizations about the best match between leadership style and the best or worst match for the situation or context (Northouse, 2013).

Other classification systems that help understand approaches to leadership research address the level at which research is conducted. For instance, Yukl (2011) proposes classifying leadership theories by the level at which they are conceptualized and applied: *intra-individual theories, dyadic theories, group-level theories, and organization-level theories.*

According to Yukl, at the intra-individual level, the traits, skills, habits, thinking, and behavior of a leader are studied. At the dyadic level, the leader-subordinate relationship and dynamics are examined. Issues of loyalty, trust, coordination, and motivation are considered at this level. At the group level, group dynamics, team-building, group learning, collective decision making, and issues of collective group identity are among the examined topics. At the organizational level, the cascading effects of leadership throughout the organization, how leaders influence the organizational culture, a leader's effectiveness in delivering on organizational performance, competitive strategy, and organizational change are some of the topics explored (ibid.). In this book, I will take a necessarily cross-sectional approach to leadership that cuts across individual, dyadic, group-level, and organizational-level leadership.

Leadership Purpose and Performance

Does leadership matter? Over the last century, the notions about leadership have evolved in such a way that scholars and skeptics have focused on the economic performance of organizations to determine if leadership matters, and if does, to what extent. The question of purpose of leadership has been addressed in depth in a seminal volume from the Harvard Business School (Nohria & Khurana, 2010).

An underlying assumption behind most scholarly and popular works on leadership has been that leadership matters primarily due to its ability to directly influence firms' economic performance. Many studies have shown a direct link between leadership and corporate performance (Wasserman, Anand, & Nohria, 2010).

Wasserman, et al., reframed leadership purpose and impact from "does leadership matter?" to "when does leadership matter?" Their research indicates that leadership does matter but is contingent on situations where opportunities are either abundant or sparse in a given industry. They studied firm performance across forty-two industries using a variance decomposition analysis and found that a firm's top leader has a statistically significant effect on the firm's performance.

The study found that a CEO's effect on corporate performance widely varies from 4.6 percent to 41.0 percent when return on assets is used as a dependent variable. Further, the Wasserman, et al., landmark study concluded that CEOs in firms with scarce external opportunities make a greater impact than those in industries with more plentiful opportunities.

Some scholars have raised serious questions about reducing leadership purpose to corporate performance (Podolny, Khurana, & Besharov, 2010). In a thoughtful and convincing examination of the concept of leadership, the authors radically reframed the meaning of leadership from economic performance to that of meaning making. They argued that "leadership research went awry when the concept of leadership became decoupled from the notion of meaning and inextricably tied to a concern with performance" (ibid., 98). Further, they declared there is a higher purpose for leadership:

> It is the role of leadership to turn an organization into an institution, by infusing the organization with values and creating a distinct organizational identity and sense of purpose that is in fact internalized by organizational members as meaningful. (Ibid., 73)

Podolny, et al., also connected the notion of leader as the source and fountainhead of organizational meaning with the bipartite framework of *transformational* and *transactional* leadership, which I will discuss next. Suffice it to say that they align transformational leadership with the ability to create meaning and transactional leadership with the ability to affect the economic performance of a firm, which is a perfect segue into a detailed discussion of transformational leadership.

TWO
Transformational and Charismatic Leadership

Scholars have used at least two criteria to define transformational leadership. The first criterion is that a transformational leader effects second-order (irreversible) change. Such a change could transform the values, mission, and the fabric of an entire organization. The second criterion is transcendental in the sense that a transformational leader rises above the mundane transactions of an organization to elevate the felt meaning of the members of the organization.

The framework of *transforming and transactional leadership* was popularized by Pulitzer Prize–winning presidential historian James MacGregor Burns (1978b), following the first usage of the concept by Downton (1973). Some leading authors on leadership (Nohria & Khurana, 2010; Yukl, 2011) have erroneously attributed transformational leadership to Bernard Bass (Bass, 1985a; Bass, 1990). In such instances of omission, the authors also failed to cite Burns, which could indicate either a disciplinary divide (between political science and business management) or a lack of attention to the topic of transformational leadership in certain scholarly circles in current times.

For me, however, Burns's work is foundational not only because of its overarching, cross-disciplinary frameworks of leadership, but also because of its incompleteness that my work hopes to address through the lens of aesthetics.

Burns's notion of leadership is directly tied to his notions of power. He contends that leadership is not possible without power. Burns ponders the intimate and inseparable relationship between power and leadership. He says, "To understand the nature of leadership requires understanding of the essence of power, for leadership is a special form of power."

Forty years ago Bertrand Russell called power the fundamental concept in social science, "in the same sense in which energy is a fundamental concept in physics" (Burns, 1978b, p. 12). Burns's classification of leadership into transactional and transforming leadership is akin to Abraham
Zaleznik's distinction between leaders and managers (Zaleznik, 1989; Zaleznik, 1993). Both Burns and Zaleznik base their binary frameworks of
leadership on psychodynamics, which may in great part explain their
characterization of leaders as change agents who push boundaries and
managers as those painting within the proverbial lines.

Leader as Embodiment of Morality

Transactional leaders, Burns observes, remain at a more or less mundane plane of trading resources of political, psychological, or economic
nature in order to govern. Burns claims there is no other higher and
overarching motive beyond the transactions and exchanges. Burns then
contrasts the portrayal of transactional (or in Zaleznik's terms, managerial) leadership with transformational leadership. He portrays transformational leadership as that relationship between a leader and followers that
transcends the routine transactions and helps both parties achieve greater
self-fulfillment. Burns says transforming leadership occurs "when one or
more persons *engage* with others in such a way that leaders and followers
raise one another to higher levels of motivation and morality" (Burns,
1978b, 20). Further, expanding on the notion of morality, Burns discerns
that the sense of morality is translated when the leaders and followers
share a set of true motives, values, and goals that include aesthetic need
(ibid., 36):

> Leadership is a process of morality to the degree that leaders engage
> with followers on the basis of shared motives and values and goals—
> on the basis, that is, of the followers' "true" needs as well as those of
> leaders: psychological, economic, safety, spiritual, sexual, aesthetic, or
> physical.

Leader as Unifier

Burns's portrayal of the key difference between transactional and
transforming leaders could be traced to the notion of *engagement*. There is
a sense of dovetailing implied in the transforming leader-follower relationship, compared to transactional leadership where there is a matter-of-
fact distance between the exchanging people. By *engagement*, Burns
means that the leaders and followers are unified by a common purpose,
playing on the same side rather than acting as weight and counterweight
on different sides in a transaction.

A common, larger, higher, moral purpose motivates, elevates, and
moves the leaders and followers together. Through engagement, Burns

observes, transformational leaders inspire followers to become leaders in their own right: "leaders throw themselves into a relationship with followers who will feel 'elevated' by it and often become more active themselves, thereby creating new cadres of leaders," (ibid., p. 20).

Leader as Guru

According to Burns, motivation is the driving force behind transformational leadership. Motivation fosters engagement, builds the team, and inspires the team and other stakeholders to pursue a higher, larger, nobler moral purpose that transcends a specific task or project. Motivation is also closely tied to the leader's ability to articulate the purpose, promote shared values, and move beyond the transactions of give-and-take and carrot and stick. Motivation taps into the followers' inner constitution and finds the energy from within rather than relying on coercion or outside incentives. The notion of *engagement* is deeply nuanced and describes a relationship that transcends the immediate task or project and operates at the level of "self-actualization" in Abraham Maslow's hierarchy of needs, to which Burns often refers in his exposition about transformational leadership:

> Self-actualization is to Maslow a complex class of "higher" needs, a need less imperative than that for sheer survival, less related to brute physical and psychological needs, a need more healthy psychologically, tending toward more creativity and a better balance between individual and collective claims, a continuing striving for efficacy in a series of challenges and tasks. . . . Unlike the more basic needs such as those for safety and affection, self-actualization, Maslow notes, is "intrinsic growth of what is already in the organism, or more accurately of what is the organism itself." (Burns, 1978a)

Further, Burns observes a relationship between the ability of transforming leaders to effect change and their ability to be changed themselves by learning and being open to being taught:

> I suggest that the most marked characteristic of self-actualizers as potential leaders goes beyond Maslow's self-actualization; it is their capacity to *learn* from others and from the environment—the capacity to be *taught*. That capacity calls for an ability to listen and be guided by others without being threatened by them. . . . Self-actualization ultimately means the ability *to lead by being led*. (Ibid.) [Italics in the original]

Burns covers a wide ground of areas of leadership in exemplifying his thesis. He speaks of political, intellectual, reform, revolutionary, and executive leadership. He holds Gandhi as a paragon of transforming leadership and carefully contrasts this style with that of Hitler, who does not meet the criteria for the moral foundations necessary for a leader. Burns's distinction between leaders and demagogues is a crucial one, which is often missed by many people. Both leadership and dictatorship are forms of power, but they cannot be equated to each other.

Leader as Psychoanalyst

Burns reaches into psychoanalysis in providing an incisive and revealing analysis of transforming leadership. He says, in one of the most powerful insights about transforming leadership, that a leader must be able to peer into the unconscious plane of the organization and bring it to a conscious plane. He wrote:

> Conflict—disagreement over goals within an array of followers, fear of outsiders, and competition for scarce resources—immensely invigorates the mobilization of consensus and dissensus. But the fundamental process is a more elusive one; it is, in large part, *to make conscious what lies unconscious among followers.* (Burns, 1978b, p. 40) [Italics in the original].

Through psychoanalytic frameworks transformational leaders "induce people to be aware or conscious of what they feel—to feel their true needs so strongly, to define their values so meaningfully, that they can be moved to purposeful action" (ibid.). Note the emphasis on *feeling* rather than *thinking* or *understanding*. In that sense, Burns is suggesting that part of the challenge of transformational leadership is to operate at a tacit, emotional, and aesthetic level more than at an explicit and cognitive level.

Transactional leadership is about trading, exchanging, and interacting with others to accomplish tasks that are economic or political in nature. Burns said:

> These actions of transactional leadership react to immediate situations and pressures, strike bargains with allies and adversaries, follow limited and short-run goals, and seek to maintain equilibrium and to avoid fundamental change. (Ibid.)

In discussing the characteristics of reform leaders who lead transformational change such as social and political revolutions, Burns finds they are usually inhibited by the "tenacious inertia of existing institutions." He observes that a combination of transformational and transactional approaches is needed to bring about enduring change:

> Reform is ever poised between the transforming and the transactional—transforming in spirit and posture, transactional in process and results. Revolutionary leaders understand this. They seek to evade or minimize transactional processes and costs—and thus they incur other costs on their own. (Ibid.)

In sum, Burns's notions of transformational leadership consist of six major elements that could be encapsulated in Table 2.1. In the table, *modal elements* are related to the process of leadership, and *end elements* address the goals of leadership:

Leaders as Twice-Born People

Abraham Zaleznik—a psychoanalyst and professor at Harvard Business School—was a towering figure whose consequential work on leadership ranks with that of Burns. Advancing another binary model of leadership, Abraham Zaleznik published a highly influential essay that distinguished managers from leaders (Zaleznik, 1977) just a year before Burns brought out his seminal book on leadership.

Zaleznik refers to William James's classification of people into two types: *once born* and *twice born*. By doing so, Zaleznik dips into the psychological makeup and development of individuals rather than their behaviors. Once-born people are the ones with straightforward life experience, peaceful, continuous, and requiring few adjustments. Twice-born people, on the other hand,

> . . . are marked by a continual struggle to attain some sense of order. Unlike the once borns they cannot take things for granted. . . . Leaders tend to be twice-born personalities, people who feel separate from their environment, including other people. They may work in organizations, but they never belong to them. (Zaleznik, 1977, p. 74)

Not only are the transformational leaders *transforming*, but they themselves are *transformed* individuals.

Most concepts of transformational leadership spring from Max Weber's concept of *charisma*. Weber portrays the charismatic leader as one who is an outsider, a leader who stands outside the bureaucratic structures and routine organizational constraints, and one who is anything but institutional. About charismatic leaders, Weber says:

> In order to do justice to their mission, the holders of charisma, the master as well as his disciples and followers, must stand outside the ties of this world, outside of routine occupations, as well as outside the routine obligations of family life. (M. Weber & Eisenstadt, 1968, p. 21)

Table 2.1.   Burns's Framework of Transformational Leadership (1978)

Modal Elements	End Elements
1. Engagement	5. Making conscious what lies unconscious
2. Leader making and team building	6. Self-actualization
3. Morality	
4. Motivation	

Weber further accords high moral ground to the charismatic leader:

> In its "pure" form, charisma is never a source of private gain for its
> holders in the sense of economic exploitation by the making of a
> deal. . . . It is the opposite of all ordered economy. It is the very force
> that disregards economy. (Ibid)

The notions of rising above the mundane and holding high moral ground
are themes that also permeated the leadership definitions of Burns and
Zaleznik.

Differing from Weber's notions of the charismatic leader, Philip Selznick advanced a notion of a leader as one who is inseparable from the
notion of organization or institution (Selznick, 1957). Selznick advances a
threefold framework of leadership that places leaders well within the
confines of organizational boundaries.

Firstly, he ties leadership to social situation. He posits that leaders can
only be understood in the context of what they are called upon to do,
such as handling communication within a group. He concludes, "a theory of leadership is dependent on a theory of social organization" (Selznick, 1957, p. 23).

Second, Selznick makes it clear that leadership should not be equated
to high office or authority or even decision-making. Leadership, he
argues, is not anything and everything that people in high office do. He
then makes a distinction between *routine decision-making* and *critical decision-making*, an idea which resonates with what Burns and Zaleznik theorized two decades later as transactional and transformational leadership. However, Selznick does *not* argue that the routine and critical decision-making are necessarily antithetical or that a single individual could
not be skilled in both. Leadership is not something that is done all the
time in all organizations.

Transformational leadership is part of the *new leadership* or *neo-charis-
matic* theories in the classification system forwarded by Day and Antonakis (Day & Antonakis, 2011). Other proponents who built their ideas on
the notion of transformational and charismatic leadership include Warren Bennis and Burt Nanus (1997), Robert Terry (1993), and Jane Howell
and Bruce Avolio (1992).

One of the criticisms of transformational leadership approaches is that
conceptualize leadership as a personality trait (something people are
born with) rather than something that aspirants could learn (Northouse,
2013). However, it is clear from Burns, Zaleznik, and others that the discourses since the 1970s have moved past trait approaches and clearly
favor an understanding that leadership is a confluence of individual development and organizational needs.

Some scholars have suggested that the link between transformational
leadership and actual transformation is a tenuous one (Antonakis, 2012).
Another general criticism of this approach is that too much emphasis is

placed on a "heroic" leader and not enough on how the followers are affected or the potential of the hero to abuse his or her charisma for destructive purposes.

The notions of leadership have clearly evolved over time, in response to the times, and as reflections of societal aspirations and conditions. The notion of leadership is as much a construct as it is a phenomenon that exists "out there." While most leadership research is concerned with political, business, or social sectors, there has been a relatively smaller volume of scholarship that addresses college and university leadership, which I will discuss next.

Transformational Leadership in Academic Institutions

Academic institutions have been described as organized anarchies (Cohen, March, & Olsen, 1972). Conditions of goal, strategy, and power ambiguity at academic institutions have been described using metaphors of circular football courts with multiple goalposts, multiple balls, and players who come and go at will (Weick, 1995). Concepts of *open* and *loosely coupled* systems have been used to describe the idiosyncratic and distinct nature of academic institutions (Birnbaum, 1988; Birnbaum, 1992).

In contradistinction to corporate and other private organizations, academic institutions are open-ended with blurry boundaries between inside and outside. Students who graduate do not become outsiders but become part of the extended family of alumni. Prestige is important and may be won by assessing the number of applicants rejected (selectivity) or the size and stability of an endowment. Elite institutions such as Harvard University, MIT, and the University of Pennsylvania currently boast selectivity rates at or below 10 percent. The mission of academic institutions is often vague and spans teaching, research, and service rather than being solely driven by one product or one niche service. Leaders in academe need to possess clear awareness of the peculiar organizational context for their leadership to be effective.

The terms *colleges, universities, academic institutions,* and *higher education organizations* will be used interchangeably here. The phrase *presidential leadership* is intended to mean university presidential leadership, an interpretation made with cautious awareness that the sizes, missions, and complexity of academic institutions vary considerably, pose different challenges to their leaders, and would require a more nuanced interpretation for a closer examination in future studies.

American college and university presidency, which has become the gold standard of academic leadership around the world, has evolved over the last three centuries (Prator, 1963; Thelin, 2004). Instituted as a break from the British models of ceremonial presidency and professorial governance, the American college presidents wielded significantly greater power than their British counterparts. The theories about academic presidential leadership are sizeable, if not as prolific as those of business leadership.

Much if not all of the scholarship on presidential leadership could be categorized, using Yukl's classification of leadership, as favoring either *the situational* or *the contingency* approach. Also, most scholarship on presidential leadership falls under transactional leadership. Relatively little writing exists that addresses the transformational potential of presidential leadership (Fisher, 1984; Fisher et al., 1988; Fisher & Koch, 1996b; Kerr, 1984; Kerr, 2001). Presidential memoirs have often acknowledged the transformational potential yet provided dire prognoses about the gradual weakening of the college presidency (Bennis, 1994; Bowen, 2011; Duderstadt, 2007).

The prevailing position held by many scholars of academic leadership is that the college presidency is a transactional job, a position that has been contested by few others (Fisher & Koch, 1996a, p. ix). Fisher and Koch characterize the transactional versus transformational leadership debate as upholding the ideological positions held by competing scholarly camps rather than an argument rooted in the reality of the world (Ibid.):

> Transformationalists generally believe in shared governance, but hold that within such a system individual accountability must be maintained and that the president is the final authority under the board in all matters. The transformational position dates back to the founding of Harvard

Fisher and Koch point out that rarely are the academic leadership models situated within the larger scholarship on leadership. The scholars making a case for transactional leadership appear to represent what Bergquist and Pawlak call *collegial cultures* in distinction to *managerial* or *developmental cultures* (Bergquist & Pawlak, 2008). Collegial cultures are cultures that strongly favor faculty autonomy. Harvard University and the University of Pennsylvania are places where faculty members hold tremendous influence and command respect from both internal and external constituencies.

In contrast, in managerial cultures, the administrators have greater executive power while faculty members are relegated to carrying out decisions made largely by the administrators.

Cohen and March's oft-cited study of presidential leadership takes a decidedly transactional tack (Cohen & March, 1986b). Basing their conclusions on the assumption that academic institutions are organized anarchies with a high degree of goal ambiguity and loosely coupled systems where the definitions of success are also ambiguous, Cohen and March argue, with a flair for drama, to minimize the impact of presidential leadership on academic institutions:

The world may collapse tomorrow; it may not. The university may survive another ten years; it may not. The differences are important, and the problems are serious. But the outcomes do not much depend on the college president. He is human. His capabilities are limited, and his responsibility is limited by his capabilities. We believe there are modest gains to be made by making some changes in the perception of his role. We believe presidents can be more effective and more relaxed. We do not believe in magic. (Ibid, p. 5)

Differing largely from Cohen and March's conclusions, other scholars such as Morrill echoed Fisher and Koch's critique that "we may be left only with administrative tactics unless we change our assumptions about the nature of leadership" (Morrill, 2010, p. 28).

The most vocal of the transactionalists, Robert Birnbaum is critical of the notions of transformational leadership or charismatic leadership in the academic world (Birnbaum, 1992). He calls the notions of transformational leadership myths and tries to articulate how those notions are either not sensible, nonexistent, or too elusive in the context of colleges and universities.

Firstly, Birnbaum brushes aside the notion of "presidential vision" as being incongruent with the way academic institutions operate, as stated earlier by Cohen and March. However, upon close examination of his argument, Birnbaum's objections stem from the assumption that presidential vision is necessarily pre-meditated, dissociated from institutional processes, and often inconsistent with the institutional culture. Birnbaum cites how three college presidents "failed to create a shared vision because they tried to create a presidential vision" (ibid., p. 27).

Birnbaum then offers a successful process of visioning by a president who "listened carefully and respected what he heard. He connected the vision to the college's history and values, and grounded it in the college as it presently existed" (ibid.). It is worth noting that Birnbaum's objections appear to be related to *how* a president arrives at a vision rather than presidential vision in and of itself.

Birnbaum portrays the notion that a president is a transformational leader as a myth. He states unequivocally "Transformational leadership, through which extraordinary people change organizational goals and values, is an anomaly in higher education" (ibid., p. 29). It is unclear, however, if transformational leadership is an anomaly because the leadership stock is inadequate (from a trait point of view or from preparation for the job), or if there is an unquestionably absolute value placed in the academic culture of an institution that makes transformational change simply undesirable irrespective of the times and context.

As most presidents rise up from faculty ranks to become presidents, the socialization process as well as the process of preparation to take the helm of a complex organization could contribute to the ability to transform. Other factors might also explain why transformational leadership is rarer in academia than what Birnbaum offers. What is evident in Birnbaum's argument is that he equates transformational leadership to unreasonable, dictatorial actions that threaten the stability and peace of an academic institution. Birnbaum cites the following conservative comment to bolster his arguments against transformational leadership (ibid., p. 31):

> The rarity of successful transformational leadership makes it all the more noticeable when it is manifest. But because it is so often related to a complex web of situational contingencies, idiosyncratic personalities, and chance events, little likelihood exists that its nature can ever be truly understood or its frequency increased. This situation is not necessarily a cause for despair, however; organizations can probably tolerate only a limited level of transformation, and the constant changes of values induced by a succession of transformational leaders would severely threaten both the stability of institutions and the systems of mutual interaction of which they are a part.

Birnbaum appears to attribute pathological compulsions to transformational leaders *en masse*. The rarity of emphatic and transformational leadership in higher education (or elsewhere) does not appear to make it undesirable in absolute terms. The transactional views of academic leadership have been contested by others who described such views as the "left wing" of academic leadership discourses and observed that academic management has changed significantly in the last four decades (Bousquet, 2008, p. 74).

Few books that explore the efficacy of transformational leadership in universities have found encouraging results (Grafton, 2009; Grosso, 2008; Head, 2009; Hempowicz, 2010; Morral, 2012). In a limited study at a private, religiously affiliated doctoral research university, Grosso (2008) found that faculty put in extra effort and expressed higher job satisfaction if they perceived the president to be transformational. Grosso's study also showed that in such instances of transformational presidential leadership, faculty exhibited the morale and motivation to transcend self-interest for the benefit of the institutional goals.

In a study of three faith-based liberal arts colleges, Head (2009) found that transformational leadership played a key role in the turnaround of the institutions and that all three presidents' use of symbolic leadership was an essential part of their leadership approach.

Hempowicz (2010) found that the vitality of Title III- and Title V-eligible private colleges (federally categorized—either by mission or by enrolled student population—as institutions supporting specific minority populations such as Native American, Black, Hispanic, etc.) was dependent on the transformational characteristics of the institutions' presidents. Morral (2012) found that transformational leadership facilitates and is positively associated with follower creativity.

Objections to transformational leadership appear to misconstrue, or transmogrify, theories and practices of leadership. Higher education institutions are complex organizations with strong organizational cultures that offer opportunities and challenges for transformational change brought about by acts of leadership. Although there have been chronicles of the lives of great presidents of yesteryear (Padilla, 2005), they remain cursory and anecdotal (Brodie & Banner, 2005; Brown, 2006; Kormondy & Keith, 2008).

Gone are the times when stasis and tradition have ruled management of academic institutions. At a time when the changing conditions of global economy, network society, and climate change are demanding responsive organizations, the relevance and need for more research on transformational leadership is paramount. Also relevant and critical is to bring to the forefront novel perspectives on transformational leadership as this book strives to do.

Transformation is not an abstract notion. Change is not an invisible phenomenon. Transformation and change are concrete phenomena that are experienced in day-to-day activities as well as periodic events such as special ceremonies. However, a majority of scholarship on leadership as well as transformational leadership has been focused on abstract notions and cognitive frameworks. The importance of aesthetics—ergo concrete sensory experiences, bodily feelings, and organizational artifacts in organizational change—has been largely missing from or incorrectly categorized as "symbolic leadership" in scholarly as well as popular literature on leadership. The primary intent of this book is to convey the need for understanding the aesthetic dimension of leadership and organizations.

THREE

Aesthetics of Organizations and Leadership

Legendary children's book artist and writer Maurice Sendak has often surprised us with his unique perspective on the world. For him, books are not just functional vehicles for conveying content but are content themselves in a profoundly aesthetic sense:

> The fresh new book smelled divine and felt even better, all shiny and smooth with a brilliant inlaid picture on the dark red front cover. Thus began my passion for books. Not reading, but smelling, fondling, biting and luxuriously caressing. (Sendak, 2000)

Maurice Sendak's vivid description of his love for books beautifully differentiates the aesthetics of a book from its textual content. The smell, sight, touch, and even taste of a book are aesthetic experiences that many people long for in a world where e-books on electronic reading devices have taken hold. We could extend this aesthetic principle to understand other phenomena such as organizations and leadership.

What are *aesthetics*? The world meets us through our senses. Our sensory experiences provide the foundations for us to construct our inner worlds. There are special experiences that touch us, move us, and engage our senses. Such encounters are aesthetic experiences that activate the senses and leave palpable and visceral feelings as well as memories. The opposite of aesthetics are *anesthetics*, when senses are numbed and memory is absent. Aesthetics could also be described as a special category of knowledge gained through sensory perceptions that helps integrate, bridge, and meld the sensory experiences through such cognitive processes as sensemaking (Eisenberg, 2006; Weick, 1995). Strati (1999b) observes, similarly, that aesthetics is a form of knowledge gained from the five senses of sight, touch, sound, smell, and taste, and by the human capacity for aesthetic judgment.

Organizational aesthetics is concerned with how an organization senses and feels itself. Strati traces the origins of organizational aesthetics to philosopher Martin Heiddegger's phenomenological expositions about the "physical nature of organizations, their concreteness of the world, and their thingliness" (Strati, 2010). Strati further defines the field of aesthetics of organization as follows:

> The underlying assumption of the aesthetic approach to the study of organizations is that, although an organization is indeed a social and collective construct . . . it is not an exclusively cognitive one but derives from the knowledge-creating faculties of all the human senses . . . This assumption has a number of consequences. First, the organization is considered as the product of specific processes whereby it is invented, negotiated and redefined by using the entire complex of the knowledge creating faculties of both organizational actors and organization scholars (Strati, 2000, p. 13).

Linstead and Höpfl also make similar observations about the scope, nature, and approach of research in organizational aesthetics:

> Over the past twenty years the study of meaning in organizations, tacit knowledge, artifacts and cultures has influenced the emergence of a concern for the aesthetic aspects of organization. However, it would be grossly simplistic to assume that such an interest is merely in the notion of beauty or elegance in the form, architecture or structures of organizations. Indeed, such an assumption would direct the field towards the development of *aesthetics of organizing* with little regard for the epistemological issues with which Strati would like us to engage. It is the very fact that an aesthetic approach to organizational studies "problematizes the rational" which makes it an important concern for organizational theorists (Höpfl & Linstead, 2000, p. 1)

Organizational aesthetics involves organizational artifacts ranging from objects such as chairs, tables, logos, colors, sounds, and dresses, to architecture and landscape architecture, which are elements that are subject to transformational change. Approaching organizational studies from the aesthetic perspective is crucial for two reasons. Firstly, organizational identity formation is a process of sensory experience as much as it is a cognitive process. Through interactions with artifacts and members of an organization, one begins to construct what aesthetics researchers describe as a "feel" for the organization (Warren, 2002). The feel includes sights, smells, sounds, and the full range of sensory experiences. Secondly, leadership, as an organizational phenomenon, is centrally implicated in the management and orchestration of organizational aesthetics, as aesthetic is, so to speak, where rubber meets the road. A consistent set of experiences in space and time is essential to conjure the "sameness" that is central to organizational identity.

Charisma and the Aesthetics of Leadership

Organizational aesthetics and leadership are both organizational phenomena. Are these two concepts related? If so, how and why are they significant? Earlier in the discussion, Max Weber's concepts of charisma were introduced (M. Weber & Eisenstadt, 1968). Virtually all scholars of leadership pay tribute to Weber's charisma either by building on it or by decrying the concept as an illusion or abomination (Antonakis, 2012; Bass et al., 1990; Burns, 1978b; Downton, 1973; Selznick, 1957; Terry, 1993; M. Weber, 1968; 1947; M. Weber & Eisenstadt, 1968). Charisma is perhaps as widely used a term as leadership.

The etymological origins of charisma provide us insight into the richer nuances often missed in the common usage of the word. The Greek root of charisma is *charis,* which means favor, gift, and grace. It is not a surprise that charisma is associated with personal talent and presence.

The concept of charisma has been considered by many scholars, from a psychological perspective, as a personality trait, as something a person possesses naturally. Rarely has it been seen through other lenses, particularly the aesthetic lens. Donna Ladkin (2006) argues that charisma could be *reconsidered* from an aesthetic viewpoint. Ladkin cites Manfred Kets de Vries, who defines the charismatic role of a leader as one based on personality traits (Ladkin, 2006, p.167):

> Indeed, representation of charisma as a much prized, individually based attribute to which leaders should aspire is a recurring refrain in the literature. For instance, Kets de Vries (2004) gives the charismatic role (as distinct from the instrumental role) a key place in effective leadership, suggesting that it encompasses "how leaders envision, empower and energize" their followers. The leadership theory recently in vogue which perhaps most relies on the notion of charisma is "transformational leadership," which suggests that effective leadership relies on personal charisma, comprised of particular skills or traits in the leader including moral vision, coupled with sensitivity to the demands of the context.

In contradistinction to such traditional understanding of charisma as a personality trait, Ladkin proposes a situational model that is relational between leader and follower. In other words, charisma is a result of followers' perception of *leader as an aesthetic experience.* It is the aesthetic sensibility of people that attunes them to the qualities of artifacts and people that they encounter. Charismatic qualities are, thus, a result of such relational, aesthetic encounters. Charisma is not a figment of imagination but a phenomenon that cannot be ignored in understanding leadership.

Beauty and Sublimity

One of the categories of aesthetic experiences is the *sublime*. It is crucial to understand this notion in order to understand the aesthetic dimension of charisma. Sublimity and beauty are distinctly different aesthetic experiences. Beauty is often defined as a set of special qualities and characteristics of artifacts and people that brings sensory pleasure to those experiencing such qualities. Such characteristics as scale, harmony, proportion, and symmetry are used to frame beauty. Sensations of pleasure are associated with the experience of beauty. There is an endearing, enticing, enthralling quality to an object of beauty.

The sublime, on the other hand, is about an overwhelming experience that defies common frameworks of understanding the experience. Cassius Longinus, a rhetorician of antiquity, has been credited with a treatise on *sublimity*. Longinus writes (Ladkin, 2006, p. 168):

> The sublime denotes the moment when the individual's affective and cognitive dispositions towards the world are subjected to a sense of displacement . . . amazement and wonder exact invincible power and force and get the better of the hearer. . . . Sublimity . . . produced at the right moment, tears everything up like a whirlwind.

Power, movement, and the ability to unsettle the person who experiences it characterize the sublime. In other words, unlike beauty, which belongs to the properties of the object, sublimity is experienced by the perceiver. Immanuel Kant, in his *Critique of Judgment* (Kant & Meredith, 1952) provides a vigorous commentary on the sublime. For Kant, sublimity has a transcendental dimension that beauty does not. There is an otherworldly quality and a sense of awe evoked in the presence of the sublime. He compares beauty and the sublime (ibid., pp. 68–69):

> The beautiful in nature is a question of the form of an object, and this consists in limitation, whereas the sublime is to be found in an object even devoid of form, so far as it immediately involves, or else by its presence provokes a representation of limitlessness, yet with a superadded thought of its totality. . . . For the beautiful is directly attended with a feeling of the furtherance of life, and is thus compatible with charms and a playful imagination . . . the delight in the sublime does not so much involve positive pleasure as admiration or respect, i.e., merits the name of a negative pleasure.

Ladkin aligns the sublime with qualities of "mightiness," "enormity," and "superiority" (2006, p. 170). She notes that charismatic leaders can elicit such feelings in the perceivers. These are qualities that unsettle and disturb and are difficult to process within the frameworks of collegiality, fraternity, and likeability, which partially explains why transformational and charismatic leadership often is ill received, particularly in the shared governance situation of higher education.

In the corporate sectors transformational leadership has garnered enormous attention. It is through the aesthetic framework that one can begin to understand the nature and implications of the aesthetics of trans-formational leadership, or simply put, *aesthetic leadership*.

Aesthetic Leadership and Symbolic Leadership

Aesthetics and symbols are often conflated or mistaken for each other. Despite the intricate relationship between aesthetic and symbolic leader-ship, it is worth noting the significant differences between those two forms. Symbols invoke what is *not* present in a given situation (represen-tation), where one thing (a leader) stands for something else. Aesthetics is about what is *present* to the senses and the sensory perception of the immediate phenomenon. It is therefore important to distinguish Bolman and Deal's (2008) *symbolic frame of leadership* from the aesthetic leadership frame. It could further be said that Bolman and Deal's fourfold frame-work remains incomplete without the aesthetic frame.

In summary, aesthetic experiences will continue to impact the organ-izational life and the phenomenon called leadership. Beauty elicits attrac-tion and positive pleasure; sublimity elicits awe and humility; grotesque-ness repulses and disgusts; tragedy elicits pain and grief; and comedy evokes hilarity and buoyancy (Strati, 2010). Charismatic and transforma-tional leaders, to examine them from an aesthetic perspective, provoke subliminal responses in the followers; it is this energy they use to trans-form organizations.

Aesthetics as Tacit Knowledge

In 1967, Michael Polanyi theorized that, like the tip of an iceberg, explicit and denotative knowledge is only a small portion of a vast amount of connotative and *tacit knowledge* (Polanyi, 1967). He observed that people "can know more than they can tell." Polanyi gives examples such as face recognition, riding a bicycle, and other forms of visceral knowing that remain tacit, which are difficult to be articulated in words and thoughts. Skills, particularly those that require the engagement of the body, involve learning and practice that build tacit knowledge but not necessarily explicit knowledge. Polanyi observed: *"All knowledge falls into one of these two classes: it is either tacit or rooted in tacit knowledge"* (italics in the original) (Polanyi & Grene, 1969).

A tennis player who jumps wildly across the court with her arms outstretched, her gait asymmetrical, and her feet in the air to hit a perfect shot is an example of how someone "knows" exactly how to tackle a ball, even though she could not have verbally or consciously explicated "how" she did it. It would take very complex mathematical calculations and considerable time to determine how the player could precisely adjust her muscular system, align her joints, position her limbs, grip the racquet, angle the racquet to intercept the ball, and complete the shot. The tennis player is praised as an artist par excellence for using her tacit knowledge. Polanyi made a powerful observation:

> The ideal of a strictly explicit knowledge is indeed self-contradictory; deprived of their tacit coefficients, all spoken words, all formulae, all maps and graphs, are strictly meaningless. An exact mathematical theory means nothing unless we recognize an inexact non-mathematical knowledge on which it bears and a person whose judgment upholds this bearing. (Ibid.)

Elsewhere, he noted:

> Our body is the ultimate instrument of all our external knowledge, whether intellectual or practical. In all our waking moments we are relying on our awareness of contacts of our body with things outside for attending to these things. Our own body is the only thing, which we never normally experience as an object, but experience always in terms of the world to which we are attending from our body. (Polanyi, 1967)

In all fields of fine or performing arts, tacit knowledge plays a big role in defining expertise and virtuosity. The way to gain tacit knowledge is, often, through tacit knowing and practice, noted Polanyi. Tacit knowing involves experiential methods of doing and viscerally experiencing the circumstances that are then internalized and repeated. Further, Polanyi notes that the "focal awareness" in totality of sensory experience in a situation is only a small part of the larger, tacit awareness gained from any given situation.

Architectural theorist and critic Chris Abel explicated the function of tacit knowing in architecture (Abel, 1981). Abel observed the intricate interconnections between architecture, identity, and tacit knowing:

> What is the role of tacit knowing and indwelling in the processes of orientation and identification with a place? It may be surmised that place identity itself is a function of tacit knowing, by which individuals come to dwell in a place not only physically but also by metaphoric extension of their own bodies. By implication, people communicate and interact with other people also in large part by making use of their architecture; much in the same way they make use of their own bodies, as the proximal term of tacit knowing. (Abel, 1981)

Polanyi's notion of tacit knowledge forms the basis for Donald Schön's notions of knowing-in-action:

> Our knowing is ordinarily tacit, implicit in our patterns of action and in our feel for the stuff with which we are dealing. It seems right to say that our knowledge is in our action. And similarly, the workday life of the professional practitioner reveals, in its recognitions, judgments, and skills, a pattern of tacit knowing-in-action. (Schön, 1995)

It is a well-acknowledged fact that universities create knowledge. The knowledge-creation mission of higher education institutions has become more prominent today than ever before; albeit, much of it is driven by the need for greater revenue from knowledge-creation activities.

Architecture of Academic Institutions

In *La Nausée*, Jean-Paul Sartre's hero Antoine Roquentin muses about the power of tacit knowledge inherent in the built world (Marcel, 1995, p. 50):

> Objects ought not to move one, since they are not alive. They should be used and put back in their place; one lives among them, they are useful and that is all. But I am moved by them, it is unbearable. I am as frightened of coming in contact with them as if they were live beasts.

The architecture of an organization is one of the foundational elements of organizational artifacts that communicates the most enduring continuity for an organization's identity and meaning (Broadbent et al., 1980; Eco, 1979; Giedion, 1967; Jencks, 1991; Preziosi, 1979; Rykwert, 1982; Strati, 1999c; Strati, 2010). Aesthetics in general and architecture in particular have been considered, in addition to their spatial-temporal structuring of activities, as a form of organizational communication (Strati, 2010). Other scholars have argued that architecture—as part of organizational symbolic systems and as the physical "packaging" of the organization—serves as the essential embodiment of organization (Alvesson & Berg, 1992). Strati observed (Strati, 201, p.165):

> Corporate architectures perform the basic communicative function, at once elementary and essential, of 'signaling a presence': the organization exists, it belongs to society, and its presence therein has a history behind it, which is part of the history of that society.

Architecture acts like a cultural flywheel. It is slow to gather momentum. But once initiated and built, buildings and cities carry the cultural patterns for thousands of years. Even when all other ephemeral manifestations of culture disappear or are absorbed by the vicissitudes of time, architecture remains as a record of the organizations and societies that gave rise to it. The transformational change of an organization is one of the most strategic ways of translating organizational identity and culture into enduring artifacts.

Gagliardi (1990) proposes that artifacts are primary cultural phenomena themselves, providing an existential foothold to human beings by defining the place and a set of coherent experiences that provide "sameness" and continuity for them (Gagliardi, 1990; Norberg-Schulz, 1980). Artifacts (such as architecture) are, Gagliardi argues, products of human actions, intentional, and perceived by the senses. Artifacts "render organizational control sensorially perceptible, in that they constitute the perceptual premises in determining the effective course of events in corporate life" (Strati, 1999c, p.159). The implication of this argument is that the artifacts and the physical environments are fundamental to and essential for the transmission of culture.

The world of higher education is replete with examples of place making that reflect the identity of institutions. However, the average tenure of university presidents, according to *Inside Higher Education*'s 2011 survey of presidents (Lederman, 2011), stands at eight to nine years, which is down from an average of eleven years in the 1970s (Cohen & March, 1986b). Thus, transforming the institutional identity through architecture poses special challenges to university presidents. It requires an extraordinary combination of aesthetic choice, strategic vision, fundraising capability, team building, choice of designers, and a sense of urgency to bring about physical plant transformation, a test for transformational leaders. Significant literature exists about campus planning, building, and architecture from the perspectives of planning, finances, and operations (Birks & Holford, 1972; Bryant F. Tolles, 2011; Bullock, Dickens, & Steadman, 1968; Chapman, 2006; Coulson, Roberts, & Taylor, 2010; Dober, 1992; Kenney, Dumont, & Kenney, 2005; Kolac, 2010; Lima, 1969; Loewe, 1998; M. Pearce, 2001; Zami, 2010). However, little literature can be found about the aesthetic dimensions of architectural transformations that university presidents could lead.

In the four decades of its scholarly existence, transformational leadership theories have been studied, tested, critiqued, and applied by hundreds of scholars and practitioners. However, in the academic leadership arena, transactional theorists have mostly brushed transformational leadership aside. At a time when society is demanding radical changes in academic institutions (Arum & Roksa, 2010; Kamenetz, 2006; Massy, 2003; Zemsky, 2009; Zumeta et al., 2011), there are gaps in our understanding of transformational leadership in colleges and universities. Furthermore, following the Vitruvian triad, leadership theories and studies have explored the functional and structural aspects of leadership from logic-rational perspectives, but hardly any substantive studies exist about the aesthetics of academic institutions and that of contemporary transformational presidents. The intersection of institutions, leadership, identity, and aesthetics promises to provide a substantial scholarly opportunity that could reveal insights into how leaders could accomplish transformational change within the cultural constraints and affordances of colleges and universities.

Springing from the foundation of transformational leadership theories, in the next chapter, I will discuss how a framework often used in the theory of architecture—the Vitruvian triad—could be applied to gain a better understanding of the role of aesthetics in organizational leadership.

FOUR

Vitruvian Leadership

Around the time Julius Caesar was assassinated in 44 B.C., architect Marcus Vitruvius Pollio was serving in the Roman military as a ballista. Vitruvius continued to serve under the eighteen-year-old Octavio, who took charge of a country in the throes of a civil war. Octavio was later given the honorific name Augustus in 27 B.C.

Octavio, the first emperor of Rome, launched the largest public building and renovation program in the history of Rome. Heartened by the abundance of opportunity for all those involved in architectural enterprise in those days, Vitruvius sought to gain the attention of Emperor Augustus by writing ten books on architecture entitled *De Architectura* (Weimer, 2008). In it, Vitruvius wrote extensively about architecture, construction, and military machinery. He said the education of an architect involved understanding liberal and physical arts. His books are the only written work of architecture from antiquity that survived the ravages of time. All the subsequent writings on architecture until the beginning of the eighteenth century referred to *De Architectura* (McEwen, 2003).

Why is Vitruvius' 2,000-year-old writing pertinent or even important to a discussion of leadership and management? What could we possibly learn from his ideas today? Certainly, Vitruvius did not imagine his theories would find relevance in the twenty-first century. The purpose of evoking Vitruvius in a discussion about leadership is that the interpretation and application of his ideas can shed new light on the field of management.

Vitruvius proposed a triadic framework of *utilitas, firmitas, and venustas* (Vitruvius Pollio & Morgan, 1960; 1914), which has proven to be foundational to the understanding and evaluation of the effectiveness of architecture. The framework can be translated into English as utility (function/efficiency), firmness (structure/durability), and aesthetics. The original Latin text is as follows (Vitruvius Pollio & Krohn, 1912):

> Haec autem ita fieri debent ut habeatur ratio firmitatis utilitatis venus-tatis. firmitatis erit habita ratio, cum fuerit fundamentorum ad solidum depressio et quaque e materia copiarum sine avaritia diligens electio, utilitatis autem, cum emendata est sine inpeditione usus locorum dispositio et ad regiones sui cuiusque generis apta est commoda distrib-utio, venustatis vero cum fuerit operis species grata et elegans membrorumque commensus iustas habeat symmetriarum ratiocinationes.

Vitruvius theorized that a work of architecture must address and satisfy all three aspects—*utilitas, firmitas,* and *venustas.* He implied that all three must be addressed simultaneously.

Venustas: Love through Aesthetics

While the first two aspects of the Vitruvian triad are easily under-stood, the third one, *venustas,* is less understood in its definition and implications. One of the best-known scholars of Vitruvius, Indra McEwen, (McEwen, 2003) has discussed the subtleties and nuances of *venustas* that cannot be easily boiled down to the popular translations as delight or beauty. McEwen writes:

> *Pulchritudo* was another word of beauty in Latin, but Vitruvius never uses it, nor the related adjective *pulcher* (beautiful) . . . whereas *venustas,* "more mundane in its associations . . . [an] immediate sort of beauty which is known through simple sense perception," translated the Greek *charis* (grace, charm), as Pliny and Elder attests. For Vitruvius,

Figure 4.1.   The Vitruvian Triad. Author's figure.

the proof of *venustas* is the pleasure (*voluptas*) it gives, which indeed anchors architectural beauty in the world of senses. (Ibid., p. 200)

McEwen further analyzes that *venustas* is more than just *charis* or a category of aesthetics. She broadens the meaning of *venustas* to include love:

> To begin with, one might recall with Cicero that *venustas* comes from *Venus*. According to Varro, Venus (love)—like proportion and symmetry, as Vitruvius repeatedly defines them—is a force that binds . . . This force is the origin of coherence, universal concord and community, wrote Plutarch . . . (Ibid., p. 201)

Love through aesthetics: a force that binds and a force that is the essential glue of building a community or any organization. Here we can begin to see that the relevance of the Vitruvian triad to leadership has a purpose and must employ the Venusian qualities to bind the organizations together.

Organizations are abstract constructs that can find existence only through a willful ordering of many artifacts, from a few pieces of paper to many large buildings. An organization that is a figment of imagination has no physical presence whatsoever and simply cannot exist. How leaders and other organizational players understand the abstract order of an organization as well as its concrete manifestation is a crucial ability that could be informed by the Vitruvian triad.

A building that is structurally strong but not functional and utterly uninspiring is inadequate and easily forgotten. It is usually easy enough to understand and evaluate if a work of architecture is functional and structurally strong. But it requires well-developed aesthetic sensibility (training of the five senses) to address the third aspect of architecture, *venustas*. For that reason, while there are some universally established principles of aesthetics, aesthetic sensibilities are in part a matter of culture (acculturation) and debate, and may not enjoy cross-cultural agreement about what constitutes beauty or sublimity or other categories of aesthetics.

Reasonable people may disagree on what is beautiful but agree on what constitutes a heightened sense of experience that each may interpret using different aesthetic categories than that of the other.

The Vitruvian framework has been time-tested and applied to not just architecture but to other areas of design. The framework can also be applied to other phenomena such as organizations and leadership. The Vitruvian triad could be extended beyond the physical arts, as shown in Table 2.

Normally, questions of function (what does a leader or an organization do?), structure (where in the administration does a leader fit?), and efficiency (has the leader or organization been measurably productive?) are posed. Rarely are the questions of aesthetics raised in these contexts:

Table 4.1.   Vitruvian Triad, Extended Themes

	Utilitas	Firmitas	Venustas
1	Function	Structure	Delight
2	Efficiency	Durability	Beauty/Sublimity
3	Explicit knowledge	Tacit/Explicit knowledge	Tacit knowledge
4	Mission	Artifacts (buildings, things)	Vision
5	Political	Scientific	Aesthetic
6	Potential	Actual	Phenomenal
7	Doing	Being	Feeling
8	Usability	Objects	Interactions
9	Leadership function and charge	Position occupied by leader in the organizational structure	How leadership is manifested as experiences
10	Quotidian or periodic	Robust and stable	Inspirational
11	Verbs	Nouns	Adjectives

Is an organization beautiful? Is the leader sublime? Does the organization build a cohesive community through aesthetics?

Institutions' Love Affairs with Aesthetics

Different works of architecture reflect these aspects to different degrees and in different proportions depending on the situation, the ability of the architect, and the sophistication of the client. Architecture needs to satisfy an extremely broad range of criteria that span political, scientific, and artistic requirements.[1] *Venustas* is the aspect that distinguishes pedestrian buildings from great buildings. Great works of architecture—such as the Parthenon, the Taj Mahal, Frank Lloyd Wright's Fallingwater, Le Corbusier's chapel of Notre Dame du Haut, Frank Gehry's Guggenheim Museum, Eero Saarinen's Kresge Auditorium or William Welles Bosworth's Building 10 (Figure 4.2) on the MIT campus in Cambridge—differ from the run-of-the-mill works of architecture vis-à-vis *venustas*. Great buildings define the civilizations and institutions in which they arise.

Institutions are special organizations that are foundational to societies and civilizations and differ in their purposes, structures, and aesthetics from other organizations such as businesses. For instance, institutions such as universities, the armed forces, and religious organizations are

Figure 4.2. MIT Building 10, column detail. © 2014 Damianos Photography. Used with permission.

replete with aesthetics. Colors, buildings, spaces, grounds, sounds, smells, and textures are all part of the aesthetic definition of institutions. In fact, institutions are unimaginable without their aesthetics.

Leaders of institutions are an integral part of the institutions' aesthetic experiences. A four-star general is a "highly decorated" soldier. Some religious leaders have an extraordinarily designed presence mediated by garments of color, form, and texture. The aesthetics of a university president are on display at graduation ceremonies where she wears a mortarboard with tassel and a velvet-trimmed robe with bell sleeves and carries an ornate mace. Even when a leader chooses a minimalistic aesthetic, as in the case of Mahatma Gandhi's simple loincloth, this choice still becomes a powerful aesthetic. Leaders and institutions without aesthetics are simply inconceivable.

Some researchers explore how the artistic sensibilities of leaders enhance their leadership effectiveness (Serifsoy, 2012). Other researchers establish firm relationships between leadership, liberal arts, and the physical arts, thereby making a case for the importance of aesthetic sensibilities for leaders (Weimer, 2008).

Leadership success has a direct relationship between a leader's personal identity and an organization's organizational identity in a way that can be experienced by all inside or outside the organization. In the next chapter, I will dissect the notion of organizational identity and how it stands at the intersection of leadership, aesthetics, and change.

NOTES

1. Therefore, architecture, as an academic discipline, could be found in all three kinds of academic settings: sciences and engineering, fine and performing arts, and liberal arts colleges.

FIVE

Aesthetics of Identity and Change

Organizational Identity

Who am I? Who are we now? What do we do that is consistent with who we are? Why do we need to change? What do we want to be in the future? These are some of the questions of identity that come up first in any process of transformational change.

An individual is an organization—the most basic organization there is—as deftly pointed out by Gregory Bateson (1972). It is not a big leap then, to extend that thought that all questions of identity refer to organizations, be it an individual or a collection of individuals. Questions of identity that apply to individuals could also be extended—to a great extent—to more complex organizations.

As counterintuitive as it may sound, aesthetics and identity are closely related concepts. Organizational identity finds aesthetic expression in ways that can be experienced by people within or outside of an organization, and leaves an indelible impression on them. Prestige is collective experience and coherent knowledge built over a long period of time through the weight of a series of mutually reinforcing and accumulated aesthetic experiences that fortify organizational identity.

The notions of organizational identity in scholarly literature are closely tied to and spring from the notions of individual identity frameworks (Albert & Whetten, 2004; Whetten, 1998). Erik Erikson described identity as a set of qualities and propensities of an individual that provides a sense of sameness amid change over time. He observed that identity is (Erikson, 1964, pp .95–96):

> [T]he capacity of the ego to sustain sameness and continuity in the face of changing fate. But fate always combines changes in inner conditions, which are the result of ongoing life stages, and changes in the milieu, the historical situation. Identity connotes the resiliency of maintaining

43

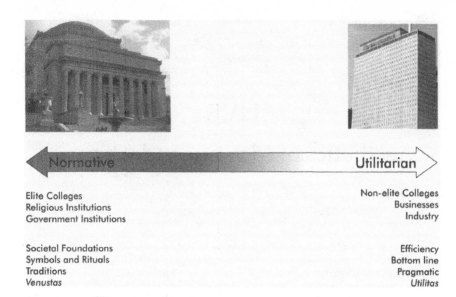

Elite Colleges
Religious Institutions
Government Institutions

Non-elite Colleges
Businesses
Industry

Societal Foundations
Symbols and Rituals
Traditions
Venustas

Efficiency
Bottom line
Pragmatic
Utilitas

Figure 5.1.   Organizational Identity Framework. Author's diagram. Conceptual framework: Albert & Whetten, 2004.

essential patterns in the process of change. Thus, strange as it may seem, it takes a well-established identity to tolerate radical change, for the well-established identity has arranged itself around basic values which cultures have in common.

Organizational psychoanalyst Michael Diamond describes organizational identity as "the means by which work groups orient themselves toward the organization and from which individuals acquire their own sense of security and identity as members" (Diamond, 1993, p. 78). Diamond describes organizational identity as a product of organizational culture. Just as understanding one's self and one's identity are important to the functioning of an individual as an individual, an organization's understanding of itself is fundamental to the functioning of that organization. However, just as an individual's identity undergoes evolution or transformation while still maintaining some elements of identity-contributing aspects, an organization, too, undergoes evolution, framing and reframing as well as transformation over time while still maintaining elements central to the character and nature of the organization.

Following Erikson's observations, one could posit that, for a transformational leader, understanding his or her own identity is important, but equally important is what the leader understands about the identity of the organization he or she leads. Many notions of leadership state that a transformational leader is one who transforms organizational culture (Albert & Whetten, 2004; Bass et al., 1990; Podolny et al., 2010; Schein, 1992;

Terry, 1993; Yukl, 2011). As an extension, it could be said that as a central element of organizational culture, the identity of the organization becomes the central concern for leadership.

Research about organizational identity is still in its relative infancy as a field (Elstak, 2008; van Rekom, Corley, & Ravasi, 2008), but there are a few frameworks that provide scholarly foundations for its study (Albert & Whetten, 2004; Whetten, 1998). Albert and Whetten advanced a three-fold framework of criteria that address character, distinctiveness, and continuity (ibid., p. 90). These are the criterion of claimed central character, the criterion of claimed distinctiveness, and the criterion of claimed temporal continuity. Further, the relationship between organizational culture and identity could be articulated as follows (ibid., p. 91):

> Is culture part of organizational identity? The relation of culture or any other aspect of an organization to the concept of identity is both an empirical question (does the organization include it among those things that are central, distinctive and enduring) and a theoretical one (does the theoretical characterization of the organization in question predict that culture will be a central, distinctive, and an enduring aspect of the organization).

The notion of the identity of an organization is not a question of the mission statement of the organization, nor is identity a well-established, understood, and consciously articulated concept of collective self. Rather, organizational identity is an often sub- or unconscious notion that comes to the conscious plane under certain conditions and circumstances. For instance, times of crisis, mergers, acquisitions, product development, long-term strategic planning, and times of leadership transition are some occasions for contemplation of identity.

An organization's identity is not only a matter of internal organizational reflection, but also a matter of perception of the external environment (such as reputation). Identity is a matter of distinction and differentiation, which means that the more precise the distinction and differentiation from the "other," the more pigeonholed an organization becomes in its environment. Placing oneself in too precise a niche has its disadvantages.

From Garages to Edifices

The next framework Albert and Whetten propose that is pertinent for transformational leaders is that of a duality between normative (such as religious and educational institutions) and utilitarian organizations (such as businesses). Normative institutions serve the larger normative purposes of the society, while utilitarian organizations serve their stockholders. However, over time—and this is where continuity over time comes to the fore—as both kinds of organizations grow and become more complex, normative institutions tend to embrace the utilitarian role (universities becoming more business-like), while utilitarian organizations aspire for a larger societal role through sponsorships to charitable organizations or by founding charitable foundations (such as the Ford Foundation).

So, what do these frameworks of identity mean for leaders? Albert and Whetten declare that the leaders of normative and utilitarian organizations must be ready to embrace both identities:

> Effective leaders of dual identity organizations should personify and support both identities. University presidents who were never professors (ordained members of the priesthood) will always be considered managers, not leaders. This deficiency should impair their effectiveness during retrenchment when they must be perceived as the champion of the normative as well as the utilitarian values of the institution. (Albert & Whetten, 2004, p. 112)

The challenge for a transformational leader is that the tasks of transformation are not merely to move the organization from one identity to another but a more complex task of addressing competing dualities (or multiplicities) of identities.

The concept of identity has been framed predominantly as a cognitive matter, but the formation, transformation, and experience of identity are aesthetic matters. Moreover, scholars using structural, human resource, political, and symbolic viewpoints have framed leadership; there is one additional dimension that has not been addressed until recently, which is the aesthetic dimension. Thus, from two perspectives (identity and leadership), there is an opportunity to explore the aesthetic dimension. Architecture is a physical and spatial embodiment of institutional identity and aesthetics and offers an opportunity to examine organizational phenomena in new light.

Take, for instance, how companies that were once formed in garages (such as Hewlett-Packard, Microsoft, Apple, Google, and many others) eventually built lavish edifices of architectural merit. In the case of MIT, a nonprofit academic institution, the campus was known until the early 1990s as "The Gray Factory on the Charles River." That utilitarian identity remained till President Charles Vest and his team of leaders transformed the campus into a normative phenomenon through sophisticated architecture.

Second-Order Change

The question of transformational or even transactional leadership is closely tied to the question of deep change. Change processes can be classified into six categories (Kezar, 2001): *evolutionary, teleological, life cycle, dialectical, social cognition, and cultural,* which extends Van de Ven and Poole's (1995) original classification of four categories. Each of these categories emerges from different disciplinary bases, assumptions, and processes. Kezar (2001) outlines a set of concepts that act as bridges between the different kinds of approaches to organizational change.

Degree of change is another concept that addresses the extent and depth of change. First-order changes involve minor, cosmetic, superficial, and non-structural modifications while the core of the organization remains the same (ibid.). Second-order change is far-reaching, structural, and transformational change, which involves transformation of values, mission, structure, culture, and aesthetic (ibid.). The most important characteristic of second-order change is that it is irreversible. Paradigmatic shifts, as the second-order changes used to be called in the 1980s, entail a comprehensive change in underlying assumptions as reflected in the transformation of all or most aspects of the functioning, identity, and operations. Changes to the graphics, furniture, color, and other similar items are first-order change and could be reversed easily. On the contrary, architecture is almost always a second-order change.

In the case of transformational leadership, it is second-order change, and in the case of transactional leadership, it is evolutionary and gradual, first-order change. Questions of change are not necessarily rational, logical processes but involve issues of basic assumptions, belief systems, worldviews, cultural frameworks, and emotions. Further, change processes are seldom value-neutral. Change without shared purpose (Pearce, 1995) cannot be considered transformational by either Burns's or Zaleznik's definitions of transformation.

Eckel, Hill, and Green defined transformational change in higher education institutions as "(1) alters the culture of the institution by changing select underlying assumptions and institutional behaviors, processes, and products; (2) is deep and pervasive, affecting the whole institution; (3) is intentional; and (4) occurs over time" (1998, p. 3).

Timing of change has special significance, according to Kezar (2001). Changes could be sudden and rapid, or slow and long. Natural changes occur over long periods of time without regard to intentionality, which could be termed evolutionary. Changes brought about by sudden events or leadership changes could be termed revolutionary according to Kezar. However, some scholars have pointed out that most change, as it falls on the bell curve of kinds of change, lies in the middle where it is neither evolutionary nor revolutionary (Levy & Merry, 1986).

Levy and Merry compiled the characteristics of first- and second-order change from a vast number of sources. The reader could consult the work by Levy and Merry for a detailed treatment of different conceptions of first- and second-order change.

First-order change is a change in one or two dimensions, components or aspects; a quantitative change (versus qualitative change); a change in content (versus context); incremental (versus revolutionary); within the old state of being (versus a new state of being, thinking, and acting) (Levy

& Merry, 1986, p. 9). Levy and Merry further summarize the stages of second-order change as observed by the scholars of organizational change (ibid., pp. 18–19). The process involves psychological, behavioral, and existential issues:

1. Denial and avoidance: Not confronting reality, building illusions, delusions, or other avoidance mechanisms such as valorizing the past.
2. Strong resistance: Where change involves probing the worldviews and belief systems of the organization's members, it is bound to arouse fear, anger, and concern of losing organizational identity.
3. Restriction: By limiting resources or attention, influential members could restrict the new paradigms and worldviews from taking root. However, the presence of restriction already signifies the crossing of the midpoint of second-order change process.
4. Multidimensional confrontation: Formation of camps, evocation of ideologies, morality, and other mechanisms of holding out could be displayed at this advanced stage of change.
5. Mourning: Letting go of the old paradigms, artifacts, and identity is perhaps the last part of the completion of second-order change.

Transformational leaders educated in the dynamics of organizational change should be able to recognize these stages of change. Institutions coasting along in ambiguous directions, goals, and controls are often cited as the reasons for avoiding second-order changes that might address legitimate reasons for responding to environmental or identity transformations (Birnbaum, 1988).

Scholars have argued that organizations are cultures consisting of patterns of meaning, values, and behaviors, which implies that organizational change involves transforming those patterns (Meyerson & Martin, 1987). Within the larger discourses about organizational culture are the cultures of academy. For transformational leaders in academe, it is essential to understand the cultural frameworks of the academic institutions they hope to change. Further, scholars have noted how institutional culture affects change process (Eckel & Kezar, 2003, p. 144). Change processes vary from industry to industry and sector to sector. Academic institutions present special challenges for change processes which have been explained by cultural frameworks.

Organizational Foolishness

One aspect of organizational change and strategy that is relevant now more than ever before is *organizational foolishness*, something that few institutions or leaders address consciously (March, 1981 & 2006). As Eckel pointed out in the foreword for this book, rationality has been consistently valorized in leadership and organizational change practices, but not the role or value of organizational foolishness. Sensible foolishness is a positive and desirable attribute of innovative organizations, and echoes what Apple's former CEO, Steve Jobs, famously quipped in his commencement speech at Stanford University (Jobs, 2005), "Stay hungry! Stay foolish!" Innovative organizations such as Apple, Google, IDEO, and MIT are known to embody and institutionally promote playfulness, risk-taking, questioning underlying assumptions, creative hacking, entertaining outlandish ideas, and possessing child-like curiosity, all of which could be summarized as organizational foolishness.

Cohen and March point out the need for college and university presidents to manage the dynamic tension between reason and foolishness in organizations (Cohen and March, 1986, p. 229):

> [W]e need to accept playfulness in social organizations. The design of organizations should attend to the problems of maintaining both playfulness and reason as aspects of intelligent choice. Since much of the literature on social design is concerned with strengthening the rationality of decision making, managers are likely to overlook the importance of play. . . . It is also a matter of making organizational structure and organizational procedures more playful. . . . We encourage organizational play by insisting on some temporary relief from control, coordination, and communication.

They conclude that the "contribution of a college president may often be measured by his capability for sustaining that creative interaction of foolishness and rationality" (ibid.). In a world that is fast evolving, the importance of organizational foolishness gains greater importance. It is not surprising that some of the most innovative higher education institutions, such as Carnegie Mellon University and MIT, do not engage in strategic planning in order to stay nimble and encourage organizational playfulness as I illustrate later in the book.

Academic Cultures and Leadership Challenges

Over the past three decades, a vast amount of literature has emerged about the notion of organizational culture from many disciplines including anthropology and sociology (Bolman & Deal, 2008; Danisman, 2010; Frank & Fahrbach, 1999; Gupta, 2011; Martin, 2001; Meyerson & Martin, 1987; Ramaley, 2002). Cultures are non-rational phenomena. Cultures are the way things are, for which there may not always be a logical explanation.

From a clinical research perspective, Schein has formulated a tripartite framework consisting of *artifacts, espoused values,* and *basic assumptions* (Schein, 1987; Schein, 1992; Schein, 1999). Artifacts are the most visible, tangible layer of the organizational world and the layer through which other more invisible layers have to be sensed, deciphered, and understood. However, Schein cautions there is no one-to-one correspondence between an artifact and other layers of the conceptual triad. Schein gives an example of how, in two different civilizations, Egyptian and Mayan, one could find pyramids. But the meaning of pyramids is very different in Egyptian civilization where they were tombs, compared to Mayan civilization where they were temples. Other scholars significantly differ from Schein.

Gagliardi (1990) challenges Schein's proposition that artifacts are tertiary phenomena that embody underlying assumptions. Rather, artifacts are primary cultural phenomena themselves, providing an existential foothold to human beings by defining the place and a set of coherent experiences that provide "sameness" and continuity for them (Gagliardi, 1990; Norberg-Schulz, 1980). Artifacts (such as architecture) are, Gagliardi argues, products of human actions, intentional, and perceived by the senses. The implication of this argument is that the artifacts and the physical environment are fundamental to and essential for the transmission of culture.

Within the larger discourses about organizational culture are the theories of cultures of academy. For transformational leaders in academe, it is essential to understand the cultural frameworks of the academic institutions they hope to change. Further, scholars have noted how institutional culture affects change process (P. D. Eckel & Kezar, 2003, p. 144). Therefore, it would be necessary to examine cultural typologies of the academic world in order for the leaders to better understand the transformational possibilities.

There have been different typologies, theories, and studies of organizational cultures of academic institutions (Chaffee & Tierney, 1988; Ferreira & Hill, 2008; Kondakci & Broeck, 2009; Lindquist, 1978; Lueddeke, 1999; Thornton & Jaeger, 2008). Bergquist and Pawlak (2008) articulated a framework of six cultures of academy. The six cultures are: *collegial, managerial, developmental, advocacy, virtual,* and *tangible* (Bergquist & Pawlak, 2008). Each of these cultures, as in Italo Calvino's *Invisible Cities* (Calvino, 1974), is not necessarily mutually exclusive but can be found in different combinations at different academic institutions.

Collegial cultures are centered on faculty and their values and assumptions. The origin of collegial cultures could be traced to the Oxbridge and German universities that eventually influenced the evolution of higher education institutions in North America. The principle of *in loco parentis* with its systems of control over the young pupils' development and environment typifies collegial cultures. Faculty has greater autonomy in collegial cultures. The metaphor that best describes collegial cultures is an idyllic and bucolic campus, a faculty heaven. Most prestigious institutions, such as the Ivy League institutions, are defined by collegial cultures where faculty members possess significant influence inside and outside the institution through their scholarly influence on campus and on society at large.

Managerial cultures are centered on managerial staff and issues. Managerial cultures value efficiency, evaluation, fiscal responsibility, and pragmatism. Bergquist and Pawlak trace the origins of managerial culture to the Catholic colleges and universities, where greater emphasis was placed on institutional controls, planning, and efficiency. Similarly, community colleges that grew out of elementary and secondary school systems carried the managerial cultures to higher education. Faculty members in these cultures have less power. They also spend more time teaching and less time doing research. The role of the president in managerial cultures shifted from being an academic head to being a manager of bureaucracy. The larger the universities, the more managerial the cultures have become, argue Bergquist and Pawlak.

The *developmental* and the *advocacy* cultures are focused on different sides of human resource development in academic institutions. The developmental cultures focus on the all-round growth and maturation of faculty, students, staff, and administrators. In distinction to collegial cultures where faculty reign supreme, in developmental cultures, there is greater inclusivity of different stakeholders, types of scholarship, and on institutional research. The developmental cultures are aligned with Peter Senge's notions of learning organizations (Senge, 1990) and Morgan's metaphor of the organization as a brain (Morgan, 2006).

The *advocacy cultures* are related to the developmental cultures in that they are concerned with human resources, but the advocacy cultures differ about the issue space, methods, and modes of operation. The issues that drive the advocacy cultures are equity, equality, egalitarianism, resource allocation, fairness, and due process. Faculty and staff unions, issues of job security, negotiations of salary and benefits, and working conditions are the elements that dominate the advocacy cultures. (Bergquist's earlier iteration of academic cultures termed the advocacy cultures as negotiation cultures.) The advocacy cultures align well with the metaphor of organizations as political systems or organizations as instruments of domination (ibid.).

The *virtual and the tangible cultures*, and their interrelationships, have tremendous implications for the physical plant of a university. The virtual culture is centered around and driven by the emerging technologies of the Internet and Web-enabled educational processes. The virtual culture is the most challenging issue for the traditional organizations that are rooted in collegial, developmental, tangible, and advocacy cultures. Bergquist and Pawlak point out that the ability to deliver education around the clock and around the globe challenges established notions of space, time, aesthetic, and relationships between the faculty, students, and the entire pedagogical past. Harvard Business School professor Clayton Christensen has written much about the potential of virtual cultures in the context of educational innovation (Christensen, 2005; Christensen, Horn, & Johnson, 2008; Christensen & Eyring, 2011).

The **tangible culture** has the prestige, legacy, real estate, worth, and power to continue to be the dominant cultural mode in the higher education world, at least for the near future. The notion of campus—its architectural power, its symbolic and ceremonial value, and its ability to serve as the locus of societal power dynamics and legacies—is timeless. Research universities continue to pour billions of dollars of strategic investment into the expansion, refurbishment, or spawning of new campuses as in the case of Cornell University's ambitions in New York City (Kiley, 12/20/2011). Tangible cultures place great importance on organizational aesthetics. These cultures also depend on creating the strongest experiences and memories for those who participate in the richly detailed spatial and physical settings.

What do these six cultures mean for organizational identity and aesthetics? How could academic leaders employ knowledge of institutional cultures to transform their organizations?

Any of the cultures could be, theoretically, found in any institution. They could be found in whole institutions or in components of institutions. They could be found in combination. In practice, however, collegial cultures would be found in elite institutions, whereas managerial cultures would be found in more utilitarian institutions such as community colleges and for-profit colleges. Tangible cultures play a key role in elite institutions and less of a role in less prestigious institutions. Organizational aesthetics and institutional identity are central matters to elite institutions and less important in non-elite institutions. All of these themes were played out in the case of the transformation of MIT, which is detailed in the next part of this book.

II

SIX

Leading with Aesthetics at MIT

In contemporary times, there is no better example of aesthetic leadership and organizational transformation than President Charles Vest at the Massachusetts Institute of Technology. MIT was transformed from a technological powerhouse that was, as one commentator quipped, "in bed with the feds" until the 1980s became a diversified institution that has reached the top rung of academic prestige and performance, thanks to a series of intentional choices made by Vest and his leadership team. This is the story of change, audacity, and deft leadership at a scale that was unprecedented in its time. As it were, the case study also illustrates the scholarly ideas and frameworks elaborated upon earlier in this book.

The Inauguration of a President

A sixty-five-foot azure blue cloth banner with maize-colored text hung from the MIT Student Center, a backdrop to the official reception following the inauguration of President Charles Marstiller Vest. The only problem was that the banner bore the colors of Vest's alma mater and read "University of Michigan at Cambridge." Vest got his first taste of MIT's culture of "student hacks"[1] at his inauguration. And he loved it. At most universities, students who played such a prank would have been disciplined, or tight control of official events would have ensured that such a hack could not have happened. That he took the hack with good humor wasn't the first tip-off that this president would bring something fresh to the Massachusetts campus.

Charles (Chuck) Vest graduated from West Virginia University in 1963 with a degree in mechanical engineering. He completed his master's and doctoral degrees in engineering at University of Michigan before starting his professorial career and eventually becoming the dean of U of M's college of engineering. In 1989, he was appointed provost by then-

Figure 6.1.   Charles Vest seen with the Hack, 1991. Courtesy MIT Museum. Photography Brian Leibowitz.

president James Duderstadt. After serving only eighteen months as provost at U of M, Vest was offered the presidency at MIT.

The circumstances under which Vest was selected as president were as dramatic as what unfolded during his presidency. Before he was even in the picture, the presidency was offered to MIT professor Phillip A. Sharp. Sharp accepted the job, but within a week changed his mind, preferring instead to continue with his research group. (He was awarded a Nobel Prize three years later, so it seems he knew his forte well.) Having exhausted the pool of internal candidates, the search committee headed by Nobel Laureate Robert Solow approached Vest in April 1990. A few weeks later, Vest was selected from an undisclosed pool of external candidates. His abilities to listen and "to draw together the faculty to reach a consensus" were cited as reasons for his selection in addition. In addition, it didn't hurt that he was an engineer and thus able to address the major engineering curricular changes seen as necessary at MIT at that time (Berlin, 1990).

As an outsider, Vest saw MIT in a fresh way. That was important for MIT, which has a long history of hiring its own graduates and faculty for the presidential post. Vest would reminisce about his initial days: "When I came here in 1990, I was an outsider at MIT. I had two or three friends in the faculty, and that was about it. I have no degree from here and never spent any time here" (Lawrence, 2006).

Figure 6.2.   Charles M. Vest. Photo: National Academy of Engineering.

Vest was to become the second-longest-serving president of MIT, for fourteen years (1990–2004), following Karl Compton, another "outsider," who served for eighteen years (1930–1948). The third-longest-serving president was also an outsider, Richard Cockburn Maclaurin, who died in office in 1920 after serving for eleven years. Presidential tenure is significant, as the length of Vest's stay gave him the time to initiate and complete so many major architectural projects, which usually take longer than a typical presidential term. Maclaurin presided over the first building boom at MIT; Vest oversaw the third.

Even before his first official day at work, Vest had become a familiar sight at MIT. He had been flying in every week for several months to listen to faculty and students discuss the future of MIT. The listening sessions crystallized for him the issues he would address upon his arrival and the task forces and committees he would immediately form. The recommendations of those task forces would in turn lead to radical changes in the nature of MIT's campus life and how the institution presented itself to the world. The president's inauguration speech revealed his approach to leadership and the moral stances that he would take later in his tenure: "Universities are not, and must never become, simply businesses. Our essence and our human purpose run far deeper than that" (Vest, 2005).

MIT at the Threshold

Vest's fourteen-year tenure at MIT can be divided equally into two phases.[2] In the first seven-year phase, he prepared the leadership platform through advocacy in Washington, D.C., by standing up to the U.S. Department of Justice. He also addressed the issues of gender equity and faculty diversity at home. The first seven years can also be described as an education in transformational leadership for him, a time when he learned significantly about the institute, its culture, its people, and its identity.

1990 was a threshold year in MIT's history. The early days of Vest's presidency were occupied with efforts to reposition MIT as a truly federally funded research powerhouse. He opened an office in Washington, D.C., and spent a significant amount of time making a new case for the role of U.S. research universities in science, engineering, and technology in the United States and the world. He built bridges with the funding agencies and rebuffed increasing competition from the likes of Stanford University and California Institute of Technology. *MIT Technology Review* covered Vest's early activities in the nation's capital (Goho, 2003):

> In the early 1990s Vest and former Hewlett-Packard CEO and president John Young (chair of the President's Council of Advisors on Science and Technology at the time), created a congressional forum on science and technology, following requests from Senator John Rockefeller (D-W. Va.) and Senator Bill Frist (R-Tenn.). The idea was that congressional "staff would become better informed," Crowley says. "They would brief their members, and this would strengthen the debate in the House

and the Senate." The forums, which are sponsored by the Council on Competitiveness, remain a tradition to this day. When Congress is in session, 200 to 300 staffers meet for a monthly lunchtime briefing to hear from leading experts on a science and technology issue the staffers select.

Vest also established a forum called Breakfast of Champions, in partnership with then-Harvard President Neil Rudenstine and a group of sixty public and private higher education institutions called Science Coalition. By 2003, they had honored thirty-five members of Congress with "Champions of Science" awards. By any account, Vest's initial years were relatively quiet on campus but were externally foundational.

Vest's predecessor, Paul Gray, for a variety of reasons, primarily fiscal, did not focus heavily on architectural issues, although the new Biology Building and a major new facility at MIT Lincoln Laboratory were fully designed and ready to go when Vest came to MIT. Deferred maintenance needs and unmet demand for new space were awaiting the arrival of Vest. Christopher Terman, a member of the building committee and a lecturer of computer science at MIT, describes how fragmented and fragile things were when Vest took office (unless otherwise cited, material from the interview conducted with Terman at MIT, on Aug. 12, 2012):

> The computer science people were all in rental space across the street and had been since 1963 when that program got started, right? The thing is we had gone from renting a couple of floors in a commercial building to now renting the entire building so just the economics of paying 5 plus million dollars a year in rent was starting to seem pretty silly because that, in fact, that was real money going to somebody else, not MIT. The Laboratory for Information and Decision Systems (LIDS) was down in Building 35. They had a couple floors in Building 35, so Linguistics and Philosophy and LIDS occupy 30 percent of the building and the computer science people occupy the other 70 percent of the research space.

Vest and his presidential team consistently deny that there was a clear starting point, a big bang, or a comprehensive vision that marked the beginning of the Vest building boom on the MIT campus. Rather, it was a confluence of a number of strands of challenges and opportunities that coincided with each other as well as the formation of a fairly comprehensive leadership team. This confluence occurred during the second half of Vest's tenure and led to one of the most significant periods of architectural change in MIT's history. The sum total of the building projects and campus development initiated or completed during Vest's tenure was over $1 billion[3] and included five major buildings totaling 1.5 million gross square feet or approximately one-fourth of MIT's campus floor space (Mitchell, 2007). Vest recalled the campus ethos regarding building just prior to the boom (unless otherwise cited, material from the interview conducted with Vest in Washington, D.C., on July 3, 2012):

> There are a lot of different things that converged, starting with the fact that I famously said somewhere along the way of my first year that I doubt if we would ever build a building while I was president, as the economy was so bad—and it was. And we ended up in fact constructing 25 percent of the campus.

The 1990s were a turning point for MIT in many ways that later influenced the physical changes to the campus. Prior to the 1990s, federal government was the single largest funding source for the institute. The proportion of federal government funding to MIT was so large that many buildings were built fully or in great part with those funds. By early 1990s, many state and private universities around the country began to aspire to more federal dollars as state funding had decreased and reliance on non-state funding increased. Thus, MIT faced increasing competition for federal dollars (Vest, 2005). Furthermore, new disciplines such as computer science became very prominent by the 1990s. By that time, one-third of MIT undergraduates majored in computer science. At the same time, previously disparate disciplines began to coalesce into new disciplines, MIT's department of Brain and Cognitive Sciences being one such example that is a combination of neuroscience, biology, and psychology.

On the surface, the changes on campus appear to have come about by chance, but Vest's leadership played a crucial role. In the mid-1990s, he was approached by a major foundation on the West Coast asking what MIT would do if given a large grant. Vest pulled together a high-powered team of leaders from different disciplines and came out with a vision that led to moving the Brain and Cognitive Sciences department to the School of Science and housing the department under one roof. Vest recalled that pivotal moment:

> So I got a group together of very senior faculty that was very eclectic; it had people like Bob Brown, the head of Chemical Engineering Department, Nicholas Negroponte, who founded the Media Lab, Michael Dertouzos, who headed the lab for computer science, Phil Sharp, who was there at that time either head of Cancer Center or Biology Department, I think probably Biology Department and maybe one or two other people . . . and kind of locked them in a room. They came back, with a very well-articulated argument [about] why the field of neuroscience was about to take off in a very new direction, why it was likely to be the most important area of fundamental science for the next fifty years, and why MIT was positioned to be a major power on this.

As it happened, the foundation that ignited the visioning process ended up not funding anything. But Vest and his leadership team utilized the opportunity to drive forward not just a couple of buildings but to strategically reorganize, blur the disciplinary boundaries, and create new opportunities. It was the push for thinking anew about academic offerings and research that spurred the need for new and different buildings. The physical plant was not a goal in itself, but a means to a larger, much more academic end and delivering on MIT's mission.

For all of its prestige as a national and international institution, as early as the 1940s and well into the 1990s, MIT had a reputation of being "the gray factory on the Charles" (Two Whole Men [Editorial], 1955; Mitchell, 2007), referring to its dour physical plant. The first big spurt of building boom in MIT's history happened around 1913, under President Maclaurin, when the institute crossed the Charles River from Boston to its present site in Cambridge. The iconic MIT buildings with two domes were designed by institute alumnus William Wells Bosworth (Figure 6.3). The second major building boom took place in the 1950s into the early 1970s when twenty-three buildings were constructed, mostly with the aid of federal grants. Terman characterized the close relationship between the government and MIT in the decades leading up to the 1990s: "We were in bed with the government, and that's what paid for a lot of the campus."

That was also the time when the MIT Chapel (1955) and the Eero Saarinen–designed Sebastian S. Kresge Auditorium (1956), the Alvar Aalto–designed Baker House (1948) were built. By the 1990s, these buildings

Figure 6.3.   MIT Building 10 (part of Maclaurin building complex) © 2014 Damianos Photography. Used with permission.

and the more than twenty that followed during this early building boom had amassed a great deal of deferred maintenance.

In 1992, upon the arrival of William (Bill) J. Mitchell as dean of the School of Architecture and Planning, Vest reconvened the campus building committee, a group that had not met for nine years.

During that time, the MIT planning office and facilities crew had been doing their routine jobs, carrying out operational, maintenance, and capital planning tasks, but no particular attention was paid at the presidential level until Vest resurrected the building committee. It is unclear if the committee was formed at the request of Dean Mitchell or by Vest himself; nevertheless, Vest saw potential for it to help identify the issues and set in motion a plan to address the maintenance backlog and pent-up demand for new projects.

By the mid-1990s, across the nation the technology boom was evident. The Internet and the World Wide Web changed the way people communicated and unfurled a new vision of commerce. Information technology industries flourished, making many of MIT's alumni wealthy and "cool," which President Vest and many other interviewees recall as a significant time of infusion of philanthropic dollars into MIT. Vest identified the IT boom as a major factor that led to the contemplation of large-scale additions to the campus:

> So the funding pattern was changing, and because of the campaign structure we began to get our primary building needs, especially the areas around computer science and engineering and around neuroscience in play. So this is the good part. The economy became enormously strong. MIT was fortunate to have very loyal alums that were a part of the growth of the IT industry. I am not quite going to say dot–com; there were not as many dot–com entrepreneurs as there were alums in the underlying IT industry. Their capacity was growing when we built a relationship with them, and that got things going well.

Thus, a confluence of external forces, internal factors, the changing world, the technological boom, years of neglected maintenance needs, and a young president who could leverage the perspective of an outsider meant that the ground was fertile for major and dramatic changes at MIT in the 1990s and early 2000s. The institute's alumni were coming into wealth at the same time technology was becoming "cool." MIT's share of federal funding had declined as a percentage of its operating budget, and the push for philanthropic dollars had, for the first time in the institute's history, acquired new importance. With the help of a strong leadership team, Vest began to address both the opportunities and challenges facing MIT.

The Formation of the Leadership Team

President Vest deeply valued the abundance of intelligence, talent, and enthusiasm among faculty, students, and staff at MIT. Recognizing fully the collegial culture at MIT, in the sense that Bergquist defined it (Bergquist & Pawlak, 2008), he considered the faculty a treasured resource. On many occasions, he placed faculty and academic administrators ahead of non-academic administrators. He believed that MIT is distinguished and well served by the unfettered voices of the faculty and students expressed in the governance structures at MIT. In fact, despite the centralized governance structure and the "strong president" model, the institute is characterized by a strong engagement and sense of ownership by faculty and students. At MIT, there was no presidential cabinet with the large cadre of vice presidents found at other universities. Vest understood this well and acknowledged how important it was for him to build a strong team of leaders:

> Another thing that I feel very strongly about for a position such as university presidency is that these things can only be done by teams and that the most fundamental thing you have to do is surround yourself with great leaders whose skills and experiences complement yours.

To that end, he described the second half of his presidency when he was able to build a "dream team" (Lawrence, 2006):

> I brought John Curry in from Caltech to serve as our executive vice president after a national search conducted by a blue ribbon committee of faculty and staff here. I knew exactly the person I needed to be our provost during this period; I recruited Bob Brown, who is a chemical engineer and has turned out to be the most talented academic administrator I have ever observed anywhere. He's just been terrific. We also hired Alice Gast as vice president for research. At this time, I had matured in my understanding of the institution. I knew where our strengths were and what we needed, so I'd like to think that we were able to build a dream team. . . . Summing up, my first effort when I arrived was to pick a provost whom I deeply trusted and felt complemented my capabilities in a variety of ways and then to let the rest of the administration evolve, but later on there came a point when I made a more sweeping set of changes in both structure and people.

In the context of such collegial culture, Vest rightly relied strongly and consistently on his leadership team, most of whom were drawn from the faculty ranks and who represented faculty interests. He unequivocally expressed his preferences in picking his team (ibid.):

> The first qualities I look for in senior administrators, even in areas like the executive vice president, are people who truly understand and care about academia. They have to have that in their blood and cherish it as a value. They have to know what faculty really does and what faculty really cares about. That is fundamental.

The core team that played a key role in the architectural changes at MIT included Bill Mitchell, Robert (Bob) Brown, Lawrence (Larry) Bacow, and in a more purely administrative capacity, John Curry, Victoria (Vicky) Sirianni, and William Dickson. The team brought a strongly academic, value-driven, and principled tenor to the presidential office. Vest was intentional and deliberate in how he built his team, and said, "Halfway through my presidency, I totally rebuilt my administration, and I did that by bringing these three people, John Curry from Caltech and Bob and Larry from inside MIT."

William J. Mitchell

On architectural matters, the most important partner for Vest and his trusted and valued architectural advisor was Dean Mitchell, who was hired as the dean of the School of Architecture and Planning in 1992. Mitchell taught for a long time at Harvard University and then at the University of California at Los Angeles. An Australian by origin, he had an unassuming demeanor that belied his oratorical and leadership skills. He could bring relentless energy and unbridled enthusiasm to any situation and advocated strongly for innovation, upholding of academic values, and the larger role of academic institutions as leaders of disciplines and of society. A brilliant and prolific writer, Mitchell had authored many books on the impact of digital design on architecture and urbanism and on contemporary culture. A charming speaker and a humble person, he spoke eloquently about the big changes occurring in the world of architecture with the advent of computational tools, techniques, media, and methods (MIT Media Lab, 2010).

At certain times in MIT's history, the dean of the School of Architecture would serve as the architectural advisor to the president. Some past deans at MIT even designed a few buildings or led the campus master planning. Notable examples include Pietro Belluschi, who designed MacGregor Dormitory, and Eduardo Catalano who designed the Stratton Student Union building in the 1960s.

Many interviewees described the strong friendship and an intellectual kinship between Mitchell and Vest. By all accounts, Mitchell was a major influence on Vest and vice versa. Mitchell would play a central role in the selection of star architects Charles Correa, Frank Gehry, Steven Holl, Fumihiko Maki, Kevin Roche, and landscape architect Laurie Olin for work at MIT. Vest acknowledged the enormous influence of Mitchell:

> We had been fortunate to attract Bill Mitchell to MIT as dean of architecture. I got to know him very well, and I was sort of doing a dual job of working with Bill and working with the normal process through the planning office and so forth for our architect selection. And I wanted to do this right. I had a lot of discussions with Bill who of course has to get all kinds of credit for what subsequently happened. And he sug-

gested a strategy that made all the sense in the world to me, and that is what we decided to use. . . . (It was) a rather straightforward process.

Vest also acknowledged the role Mitchell played in educating him on architectural matters:

I did actually appoint Bill Mitchell as the architectural advisor to the president, which was an appointment that had been made a few times in the past. So Bill played a very direct role, and all this was for me as much of a learning experience as it was a leadership experience. Bill had a big impact on this, but he did so as a teacher.

Mitchell went on to write a book that recounted the architectural dimensions of physical plant changes at MIT under Vest (Mitchell, 2007). Mitchell was also the "client" for the Media Lab building which was designed by Fumihiko Maki (in partnership with a local architectural firm Leers Weinzapfel), and opened around the time of Mitchell's untimely death in 2010.

Robert Brown

A longtime faculty member and a chemical engineer by profession, Bob Brown became the dean of the School of Engineering in 1996. He inherited an important part of the development and execution of the architectural projects under Vest, particularly the Stata Center that housed the largest academic group in his school. Brown took part in the visioning exercise that Vest conducted in response to the West Coast foundation's invitation as mentioned above. Brown went on to become provost in 1998 and president of Boston University in 2005. Vest felt that Brown "would have a more pragmatic approach than I would have," and knew he could entrust Brown with the major responsibility of heading up, initially, the Stata Center's client team, and later on, oversight of all the architectural projects. Vest acknowledged the key and complementary role Brown played in the architectural change at MIT: "Bob Brown will and should take a lot of ownership of this process with the building because he spent a lot of his time, much more hands on than I did." Vest noted that Brown "has turned out to be the most talented academic administrator I have ever observed anywhere" (Lawrence, 2006).

Lawrence Bacow

At MIT, a special position reporting to the president, called "chancellor," was used at times during the institute's history. During Vest's tenure, this position could be dubbed the chief student affairs officer who oversaw the deans of graduate and undergraduate education, a combination rarely seen at other institutions. Vest appointed Larry Bacow as chancellor in 1998. Bacow was charged with "all things student," including student life and academic outcomes. Prior to his appointment, he was a graduate of MIT, a faculty member in the School of Architecture and Planning, and acted as the elected chair of the MIT faculty. He was also a co-founder of the MIT Center for Real Estate. As chancellor, Bacow was put in charge of providing overview for the design and construction process of Simmons Hall, which housed freshmen and other undergraduates, a major cultural change at MIT that will be addressed later in this case study. Bacow served as the third chancellor of MIT until 2001, when he was selected as president of Tufts University. Bacow confirmed what many of the interviewees and other sources repeatedly observed, that Vest inspired, mentored, and led a team of highly motivated leaders (unless otherwise cited, material from the interview conducted with Bacow in Cambridge, Mass., on Sept. 13, 2012):

> One of Chuck's great strengths as a president is that he had a great nose for picking really good people. Five of his folks have gone on to run major research universities. And the people who sat around that table at Academic Council were the most talented group of people I have ever worked with, just extraordinary people on both the academic and the administrative side. And he had a way of inspiring people and laying out broad brushstrokes of what he wanted to do.

Victoria Sirianni

Vicky Sirianni, another member of Vest's core team, was a longtime employee of MIT. She was promoted to director of physical plant in July of 1993 as it was becoming evident that the magnitude of architectural issues was growing. She eventually became MIT's chief facilities officer and oversaw the third major building boom in MIT's history. Vest recalled how he depended on her to pull together all things construction: "Vicky was really the person on the ground who had to make all this happen. I just think the world of her. It was very hard on her—it was a tough period. I feel really badly about that. I certainly did value her."

John Curry and William Dickson

Two other individuals played major roles on Vest's team. William Dickson was the senior vice president to many presidents including Vest. He was often described as one of the most knowledgeable people about MIT and the person who built most of MIT since the 1960s. He was instrumental in helping Vest set many of the building projects in motion.

Dickson retired in 1998, giving way to the hiring of John Curry. Curry was the vice president for business and finance at the California Institute of Technology and one of the proponents of responsibility centered management in higher education (Strauss & Curry, 2002). He knew Vest from their undergraduate days together at West Virginia University and was

pleased to rejoin Vest at MIT as his executive vice president. Curry oversaw all operational units including finance, facilities maintenance, planning, and expansion at a time when the construction cranes hovering
above MIT seemed to outnumber the birds in the sky. Curry brought
tremendous discipline and control over new architectural projects and
coordinated the different client teams for the projects. Curry recollected
how he was inspired and engaged by Vest (unless otherwise cited, material from the interview conducted with Curry in Cambridge, Mass., on
Sept. 11, 2012):

> I got a call from Chuck, and he said, "I think I have a job here which
> may be the best in country for someone like you. Would you like to talk
> to me about it?" Well when Chuck Vest drags you out of your Pasade-
> na swimming pool in the middle of the summer, you do say yes. It was
> not only Chuck Vest, someone I admired; he was the president of MIT,
> a place I admired. So, I joined his administration in 1998. He said two
> things were the big jobs for the new executive vice president—it was
> basically covering the financial bases of the campus as well as the oper-
> ations of the campus that included facilities. He said we are going to
> return to our original roots at MIT and seek innovative architects. He
> said we have a lot of building to do, and we are behind. We haven't
> built much in recent years. We have come out of the early 1990s reces-
> sion, and it is going to be a very exciting time, and along with that we
> need a good financial plan because we are spending a lot of money,
> raising a lot of money, and probably borrowing a lot of money, and we
> have to be confident with our board that we can afford this, and we are
> staying on track. Well, the combination of financial modeling and
> building exciting buildings was too much to keep me in sunny South-
> ern California.

Thus, by 1998, eight years into his presidency, Vest had assembled an
entirely new team, heralding what some at MIT described as a "remarkable time."

Ray Stata and the MIT Corporation

Another important part of the team that raised significant funds for
the Institute was the MIT Corporation, which is its board of trustees. The
board was chaired by Paul Gray (past president of MIT and Vest's predecessor) between 1990 and 1997 and by Alexander V. d'Arbeloff between
1997 and 2003. Influential board members at that time included Ray Stata.
At MIT, there is an unusual relationship between the president and the
nearly seventy-member corporation. The executive committee consists of
nine members, the president, the MIT treasurer, and the corporation
chairman. It is a tradition that the past presidents serve as life members of
the corporation, thus retaining the continuity of experience and institutional expertise rarely seen at other universities. Moreover, the corpora-

tion members, most of whom are MIT alumni who went on to establish high technology businesses, and many of whom hold patents and other intellectual distinctions, have been characterized as different kind of members compared to trustees at any other university in the nation. Sirianni said this about the corporation (unless otherwise cited, material from the interview conducted with Sirianni at MIT on Sept. 11, 2012):

> I have worked with other institutions where trustees go into the boardroom and pump themselves up to get contracts. At MIT, it is just the opposite. I don't think anyone in the corporation gets work here at all. It's the glory! I really liked a lot of the corporation members. They were people who had been extraordinarily successful because of their brains, not making money on the backs of other people like Andrew Carnegie. These people used their brains, and they simply wanted to give back.

Although some trustees wanted inexpensive and dull buildings, Vest was persuasive enough to get a majority of them to accept the notion of innovative architecture. Curry characterized the process as a challenge:

> There were some people literally who thought we should be building very low-cost pedestrian buildings. Some of them were the trustees, and that was not easy. Chuck took serious risks in dealing with these trustees on that issue.

The partnerships that Vest would forge with the members of the corporation—and, with their support, raise $1.7 billion and approximately 250 million in bonds to back the building projects (that will be discussed later in the book) as well as other major initiatives—were crucial to MIT's strategy at that time. Most of the funds were meant for the physical facilities (MIT News Office, 2001; Wright, 2003).

It is not only what a president does that is important, but also what he chooses not to do. Once he fully recruited his team and delegated to them the responsibility of overseeing the projects, Vest stepped back from the day-to-day managerial operations of the projects and focused on resolving conflicts, addressing major setbacks, making the key decisions of choice of architects and investments, and ensuring that, despite all difficulties, the projects moved along to completion. Vest considered these experiences personally transformative:

> Now, as we got into actually building the projects everything went south. We had the last big recession, and that recession was very difficult for us, particularly in terms of campus development because not only was the economy going down, unfortunately there were two huge federally funded programs in Boston, namely, the Big Dig and the Convention Center that kept the costs of subcontractors and so forth from declining like rest of the country. So we had these big problems both pushing in the wrong direction for us. It was during that period that I have to tell you I just found an ability to persevere that I did not know that I had. If there is one thing I would have to personally—as

opposed to collectively—take responsibility for, I think it was grabbing on to the ankles of trustees like a turtle and not letting go until I got through the thing.

Bacow recalled, "Chuck challenged all of us and said that MIT should have a campus that's as creative as the people who occupy it which led to the substantial investment in architecture." Bacow further recalled how Vest mentored him and made insightful observations about his leadership potential:

We all watched what Chuck did. He was very forthcoming with advice. He was very supportive of each one of us when we were thinking about leaving (for leadership roles elsewhere). . . . I had really avoided academic administration. While I had been tapped to be chair of the faculty, that's not purely an administrative role. Nobody reports to chair of the faculty, and I had avoided being a department chair or a dean. When I became chancellor, I remember at one point we were discussing some decision, and Chuck turned to me and said, "You're a lot like me," and I said "What do you mean, Chuck?" And he said, "You will be a better president than you will be a provost."

Stephen Immerman, the current president of Montserrat College of Art, was the executive director of enterprise services and associate dean for student life at MIT during Vest's presidency. He articulated the team dynamic and the excitement at MIT at that time (unless otherwise cited, material from the interview conducted with Immerman in Beverly, Mass., on Sept. 11, 2012):

The things I remember about Chuck are that he was just and very principled. It didn't matter who you were, and he was respectful of everybody. Even if he disagreed with you, I mean you knew it, but you knew it wasn't about him. I mean ultimately we all have ego, but it really wasn't about him. He truly viewed it as service. He assembled a team around him during the second half of his presidency, his second seven or eight years, and with Bob Brown, Larry Bacow, and John Curry, and we all knew, absolutely *knew it was never going to get better than this*! And I think that's absolutely still the case! It was a wonderful time: people worked together, they were thoughtful, always solved problems together.

Other interviewees communicated the same sense of mentoring, respectfulness, boldness, collaboration, and engagement. Sirianni noted, "He called me—and I was in a meeting with Bob (Simha), and he was looking for both of us. So we both got on the phone, and he said, I respect your opinion—Chuck was always very, very cordial—but this is what I want to do, this is what I am going to do, and I am relying on the two of you to make it work."

Ray Stata, MIT's trustee and along with his wife Maria, the main donor of the Stata Center, echoed similar observations about Vest's leadership and the sense of trust and confidence he elicited (unless otherwise cited, material from the interview conducted with Stata in Norwood, Mass., on Sept. 12, 2012):

> Is this a person with whom you want to be in the boat when you are going through troubled times? And when you say something, is it sincere? Is it real? Is it honest? Is it believable? Vest is just a great leader. He's not a firebrand, you know, the type of huge persona of charisma. But when he speaks, he always speaks with wisdom. He always speaks in ways that give you trust in his integrity, in his vision, and in his judgment.

Brown, current president of Boston University, was dean of engineering and later provost of MIT. His observations about Vest's leadership are consistent with what other interviewees noted (unless otherwise cited, material from the interview conducted with Brown at Boston University on Sept. 11, 2012):

> Chuck is a very marvelous leader, but he is also a quiet leader. You won't see Chuck in many cases giving a long twenty-minute discussion of why he is going to do something. It was not made in the room in front of everybody, which stylistically would have been my style, but not Chuck's style. He listened quietly to all the pros and cons.

Laurie Olin, a prominent landscape architect who worked extensively on MIT campus projects, interacted with Vest and his leadership team on many occasions and shared Brown's observations about Vest's leadership (unless otherwise cited, material from the interview conducted with Olin in Philadelphia, Pa., on Feb. 22, 2013):

> Chuck was a man who had a vision. He was genuine. He was generous. He listened to people. He would engage you. He was happy if you would argue. . . . I mean Chuck had a great backup team. He picked good people that were strong. One of the ways you evaluate leaders is if they pick people who are weaker and then they push you around or if they pick people who are strong and might be good at their own job. And Chuck was unafraid of picking people, the strongest people, and having them around him.

Bacow remembered how Vest motivated his team and allowed them to be creative and think big:

> Chuck encouraged us to dream about how to make MIT a better place. Bill Mitchell, Bob Brown, John Curry, Vicky Sirianni, I mean I could go down the list, other deans, who were all dreaming . . . it lifted everybody's expectations.

Thus, Vest chose his team well, supported his team well, mentored well, and engendered a strong sense of personal trust and confidence in his leadership abilities. Vest delegated to his team members drawn from the academic side of the institute and put them in charge of the projects by appointing them, to the scorn of a few non-academic administrators, as leaders of the client teams for the major building projects. Vest's team choices won him strong support from the faculty and students alike and helped neutralize polarity between administration and faculty that is typical and widespread at other institutions.

Humanizing the Campus

The intersection of a student's death and a critical examination of the status of women faculty at MIT led to President Vest's recognition of architecture as a part of the solution to the institute's changing culture. As is often the case, significant and dramatic incidents trigger sea changes. A key incident at this time, a student's death, dramatically sped up a cascade of major cultural and architectural changes already underway on campus.

In the fall of 1997, when Scott Krueger arrived as a freshman, he joined a fraternity across the river from MIT, Fiji (Phi Gamma Delta). Before 2002, freshmen at MIT were not required to live on campus. Fraternities, sororities, and independent living groups were the first choice for many undergraduates rather than living in campus residence halls. On Friday, Sept. 26, 1997, at Fiji, freshmen were linked up with their new big brothers and celebrated the occasion with alcohol. Later that night and in the early hours of Saturday, Krueger was admitted to a hospital unconscious and suffering from alcohol poisoning. He remained in a coma for three days before dying. The incident proved pivotal not only for the Krueger family but also for MIT and Vest.

In 1996, coincidentally a full year before the incident took place, Vest had formed a Student Life and Learning Task Force in response to a series of student suicides and other issues of campus morale. Sirianni recalled the troubled times with a vivid image: "There was this idea about MIT students holing up in their little holes in their rooms and jumping out of the windows or drinking themselves to death."

The task force was charged with "a comprehensive review of MIT's educational mission on the threshold of the twenty-first century." With Krueger's death in 1997, the task force's role became central to an introspective examination of the education and culture of MIT. In forming the task force, Vest tapped into a tradition of MIT, as he had with the resurrection of the position of chancellor, which would allow the organization to conduct some soul searching. In 1949, President James Killian created a Committee on Educational Survey, also known as the Lewis Commission, in the face of the then dramatic changes in the American higher education world. In evoking that tradition, Vest tapped into the cultural patterns of MIT to enable critical self-reflection.

The Student Life and Learning Task Force came up with many recommendations, the most crucial being that all freshmen should be housed on campus in residence halls. The task force also recommended the development of campus facilities for freshmen and other undergraduates that would create an environment of greater responsibility and oversight by MIT. Vest accepted the recommendation and initiated measures to accommodate all freshmen in MIT facilities.

The process of healing in the aftermath of Scott Krueger's death concluded with a face-to-face meeting between Vest and Krueger's parents in the fall of 2000. Vest traveled to Orchard Park, New York, for a formal mediation session—supported by MIT's counsel, the law firm of Palmer and Dodge—and personally met with, listened to, and apologized to the Krueger family (Vest, Sept. 8, 2000; Wright, Sept. 20, 2000). The MIT News Office announcement stated (ibid.):

> Leo V. Boyle, the Krueger family's attorney, said the agreement was reached "in a powerful, honest, emotional and healing face-to-face meeting recently outside of Buffalo, NY, between the Kruegers and MIT President Charles Vest."

The Kruegers' family attorney would later credit Vest for his sincerity in facing one of the worst situations any president could imagine—to face the parents of a student about the death of their child (Wright, Sept. 20, 2000). Darlene and Robert Krueger felt that Vest's openness to meet with them in person to understand their plight with all sincerity and to provide a public as well as personal apology was genuine and moving. As a result, the Kruegers concluded the matter with a $6 million settlement out of court, significantly less than might have occurred. Of the $6 million, $1.25 million was established as a scholarship in the name of Scott Krueger. Some interviewees cited this difficult moment as a resounding demonstration of Vest's character, ability to take risks, courage, and integrity.[4] Vest marked the emotional milestone as an important point in the institute's history (Wright, Sept. 20, 2000):

> Scott's death galvanized us to action. It impelled us to greatly intensify our consideration and accelerate our actions with regard to alcohol, our housing system and other issues of student life and learning. Starting in 2002, when additional housing has been constructed, all of our freshmen will be required to live for their first year in residence halls. Our approach to alcohol education as well as to policies regarding its use — and their enforcement—has been greatly strengthened. We are building a stronger sense of community and community responsibility. All this takes longer than I would like and will never be perfect, but MIT is, and will be, a better institution for having undertaken substantial change.

It is worth noting that Dean of Science Robert Birgeneau (later to be chancellor of the University of California at Berkeley), with Vest's strong concurrence, had also commissioned a comprehensive "Study on the Status of Women Faculty at MIT's School of Science" in 1995. Biology professor Nancy Hopkins chaired the study and a subsequent follow-on. This study had parallels to the Student Life and Learning Task Force and would have dramatic impact on the architectural choices made by Vest later in his tenure. His transformative initiative about the status of women at MIT is now a well-noted phenomenon in books on leadership studies (Ancona, 2012):

> While a committee of female faculty members highlighted the need for change, President Vest set about conducting hundreds of interviews, often by referral, to help build his map of the institution. When he heard that women were discriminated against within the faculties he reviewed the data and addressed the problem in a "just do it" fashion that helped him secure an early and meaningful victory to build upon.

Bacow observed that MIT went through profound changes under Vest, particularly with respect to the demographic and cultural shifts in the organization. As an MIT alum, he noted that, prior to the 1980s, MIT was a male-dominated place where women were marginalized. All of that changed around the time of Scott Krueger's death, albeit not necessarily only because of that incident.

He noted that there were a few reasons the MIT undergraduate men lived across the Charles River, which many dubbed "the moat" that separated mentally and physically the residential life from the rigors and demands imposed by the faculty of the "Factory on the Charles." Another reason the men lived in Boston was access to socialize with women. Bacow observed:

> It used to be; if you asked the way MIT is organized is that the vast number of the fraternities were located in Boston across the river. Why? Two reasons: One is that MIT originally was located in Back Bay, in Copley Square. The older fraternity started then, but second, the women were located in Back Bay as well. There were no women on the MIT campus. As the campus evolved, what evolved with it was the need for a social life on campus on weekends. MIT used to empty out on weekends because all the guys would go where the women were.

President Vest observed an important change in the campus life at MIT brought about by admitting more women:

> The good part is, through the leadership of several presidents and obviously many other people as well as social trends, the student body and faculty became tremendously diverse from what it had been. There was a huge impact on MIT's culture because by the time I got there our undergraduate population was over 33 percent women. By the time I left it was in the upper 40 percent pushing against 50 percent. This just simply changed everything because you had a campus that was largely dependent on fraternity that we called independent living groups, and most of them were in Boston physically diverse from the campus. There was a great value in this for many people who came to MIT quite

young, often not being particularly well socialized, being very focused and so forth and through these small living groups they found a lot of support and nurture and strength. So we kind of built this culture that was dominated by the way things used to be then it got colored quite dramatically by the '60s and '70s by this sort of radical era, and there was still a lot of residue from that, and the way that the various living groups and including those in the dormitories thought about themselves, so there was a sense in which—particularly for our undergraduate culture, there was not a sort of deep feeling of all being a part of the institution called MIT.

Vest pushed the initiative to examine the status of women faculty further than any of his predecessors had. The arrival of greater numbers of women students and faculty had fundamentally changed the nature of place that was male dominated, gritty, and industrial in character. Bacow noted that the arrival of women "humanized the campus." The implications of humanizing the campus would have significant repercussions for the aesthetic and programmatic choices made by Vest's team.

The intersection of the Krueger incident and the examination of the status of women faculty was addressed through two major architectural projects—Simmons Hall and Zesiger Sports and Fitness Center, both of which were charged with supporting students and their families' social lives on the MIT campus. Vest knew that humanizing the campus would take more than putting up a residential hall:

I had already been pushing to get the athletic center done because I thought that if we were going to have all freshmen living on campus, we need to dramatically upgrade the quality of student life. So, one should look at the Zesiger Center and Simmons Hall as part of a piece of the development of the West Campus.

Residential life, sports and fitness activities, cultural activities, food courts, childcare centers, public spaces, and a greater demand for "people spaces" than the older "equipment spaces" all converged in the 1990s. Vest was the nerve center, by all accounts, of these initiatives.

Transforming the Gray Factory

In the initial days of his presidency, as he jogged along the Charles River in the mornings, Vest would notice the contrast between the stateliness of architect and institute alumnus Welles Bosworth's neoclassical buildings with their domes, and, on the northeast side of the campus, dark and rundown buildings with little character, lacking any architectural dignity that signified the top-tier academics of the institute that was behind it. Some of those who had been immersed in the institution for a long time were probably far less riled up by such contrasting sights, but for an outsider looking freshly at MIT, the stark inconsistencies between the status of MIT as a world-class institution and its physical environ-

ment were obvious. Vest also felt that neither the stateliness of Bosworth's buildings nor the industrial buildings of north side of the campus
properly reflected the "extraordinary and forward-looking reality, excitement, and electricity of what went on inside" (ibid.). In other words, Vest
clearly noticed a disconnection between the identity of the institution and
its physical manifestation in its architecture.

Coming into his presidency as an outsider, Vest was shocked by the
gritty, gray, and industrial place fit for equipment more than for people
(Joyce & Gehry, 2004):

> From the top floors of the adjacent Marriott Hotel, I could look down
> on MIT and see an unbroken rectilinear layout that somehow instantly
> made me think more of a naval base than of a campus for such a
> wonderful academic community. I also confess to a depressed feeling
> upon driving down the tired, treeless Vassar Street at the back of the
> primary campus, where steam plants, decaying buildings, and the
> nearly dilapidated and dismal gray-shingled Building 20 flanked the
> street. This was MIT's back door—its northern edge.

Vest, however, also commented that the south side, with its iconic
MIT buildings designed by Welles Bosworth on the banks of Charles
River, was spectacular.

The attitude of MIT toward its physical environment from the beginnings of its Cambridge campus in 1916 to the rapid growth in the 1960s to
the brutalist structures of later years was to maximize what was termed
as "equipment space" with tight floor-area ratios that satisfied the federal
funding agencies footing a lion's share of the cost of construction. Vest
noted:

> Obviously we have the original iconic structures. We have Baker
> House and a few wonderful things like that, but, like so many institu-
> tions, a lot of building going on through a pretty architecturally bleak
> period . . . very few public spaces. I was forever getting complaints that
> there are no places to sit down, no place for having conversations.
> Being good engineers and so forth we filled every possible corner with
> places to get our work done in a laboratory sense. There was to me, and
> I hope I am not overusing that, there is a little bit of physical weakness
> to much of the institution. Fortunately this was all counterbalanced by
> the fact that if you walk down any hallway you can feel the electricity
> and the excitement of people. I think we made up in that spirit for what
> we maybe lacked in the physical surroundings we had.

Vest's presidency was crucial as it occupied the pivotal point when
MIT's dependence on federal funding had declined, private giving
needed to be nurtured with greater intentionality, and the arrival of more
women and families increased the academic and social life of the institute. The shift in the source of funds was, then, reflected in the aesthetic
and programmatic choices of architecture under President Vest.

Vest wrote extensively about the circumstances and processes that led to MIT's third building boom. Consistent with the complexity, diversity, and messiness of the academic institution that MIT is, Vest painted a picture of ordered chaos and an extraordinary engagement of many people in the process of identifying projects, selecting architects, finding funding, and seeing things through. (Vest, 2007):

> Great universities evolve intellectually, socially, and physically rough-ly 50 percent by planning and 50 percent by serendipity. An academic institution is not like an orchestra with a president as conductor. MIT is more like a jam session among a lot of talented musicians who listen to each other and get into the flow. The president, provost, deans, and other administrators strive to hire the right "musicians," draw the themes from the evolving music, and keep the beat going. The art lies in recognizing newly emerging intellectual areas as strategic opportu-nities and moments and forging the institutional momentum and re-sources to bring vision to reality. It was in this context that MIT's cam-pus was imagined and then transformed as it passed from the twenti-eth century to the twenty-first.

Although Vest predicted in his initial days that he would not build a single building during his tenure, he ended up changing MIT "as radical-ly as Rome under Septimius Severus" (Mitchell, 2007).

Insiders and Outsiders

As with any major institutional change, unpleasant surprises and con-flicts worked their way into the process. Two blocs squared off at times. One side consisted of "insiders," conservatives who had been with the institution for a long time. They preferred to hire alumni architects known through their prior work on campus who could be trusted to keep buildings within a fairly consistent image, to keep costs manageable, and to produce predictable results. The conservatives said alumni architects had a greater understanding of MIT culture and needs than outsiders. Implicit in the argument for hiring alumni architects was the notion that nonalumni architects would be less capable of respecting MIT's past and its culture and thereby disrupt the continuity of patterns of MIT's past.

Then there were the "outsiders," including Vest, who were relatively new to the campus or otherwise progressive in their views. The outsiders saw the opportunities as another historical turning point for the institute. They relished the idea of making innovative and exciting architectural statements and creating more nuanced social environments that reflected the "boldness and audacity" that they claimed MIT stood for. Contrary to the insiders' views, Vest, as early as his inauguration time, called upon the higher instincts of MIT's constituents when he said that "to draw boundaries around our institution, to close off the free exchange of education and ideas, would be antithetical to the concept of a great university" (Vest, 2005).

While the conservative insiders looked to the past and valued continuity, the progressive outsiders looked to the future and took calculated risks in promoting experimental architecture and introducing change. The tensions between the two groups constituted many conflicts during the course of the physical campus changes.

The Risk-Taker

President Vest made no secret of his risk-taking stance with respect to architectural choices. He had been consistent about his reasoning behind the architectural choices:

> It was not that we had not done some distinguished building before, not a lot, but it had been done, but I was attracted literally to the risk-taking. I thought this is what people here do day in and day out. They take risks and try to move the boundaries out further than anybody else has. If the direction is unusual, so much the better. So it was that more than anything that attracted me to try a different kind of an architect than we have had for a while.

In fact, the words that recurred in many of the interviews characterized Vest's choice of architects and architecture as audacious, bold, innovative, risk-taking, experimental, brilliant, significant, remarkable, and exciting, all of which referred to the aesthetics, the identify of MIT, and to something larger and personally or institutionally meaningful. Some went on to describe the conflict between conservative and progressive elements as the "battle for the soul of MIT" (Mitchell, 2007).

The conservatives, on the other hand, described Vest's choices as crazy, misguided, wasteful, unaffordable, mismanaged, extravagant, and a break from MIT's traditions. Their preferred language consisted of words such as preserve, continuous, vigilant, effectiveness, careful, rational, and constancy. The MIT traditionalists favored uncontroversial and safe choices. One critic, Boston University's outspoken former President John Silber, was so incensed by what he saw across the river at MIT that he wrote a polemical book, contemptuously entitled *Architecture of the Absurd: How "Genius" Disfigured a Practical Art* (Silber, 2007) decrying Vest's architectural choices as well as slamming star architects Frank Gehry and Daniel Libeskind. For aesthetic effect, ironically, the book features Gehry's Ray and Maria Stata Center on its cover, thereby tacitly acknowledging the power of Gehry's work. Architectural critic Robert Campbell disagreed with (in fact, ridiculed) Vest's notion that the new buildings should be "audacious metaphors" (Campbell, June 19, 2007). Campbell wrote:[5]

MIT's then-president, Chuck Vest, egged on by the dean of architecture and planning, Bill Mitchell, announced another Stata mission as follows: "I believe that the buildings at this extraordinary university should be as diverse, forward thinking, and audacious as the community they serve. They should stand as a metaphor for the ingenuity at work inside them." As a principle, I regard this statement as moronic nonsense. It's like saying Einstein should have worn a crazy hat to express the fact that his brain was thinking audacious things. But many of the scientists disagree with me. They want to be in a building that proclaims how special they are . . .

Some at MIT were vehemently opposed to hiring architects Gehry and Holl and did not hesitate talking to national press (Chamberlain, 2004):

Speaking on the condition of anonymity, he blames MIT administrators who think they're experts and never allowed the project to be properly vetted by professionals. "Senior administrators should not be in charge of building," he says. "It's a terrible combination of hubris and ignorance."

Then there were believers who steadfastly stood by Vest. Sirianni described her experiences of interacting with her counterparts from the Ivy Plus universities as one of dismay and disbelief about the kinds of architectural choices being made by Vest. Further, Sirianni gave an emotional account of Vest's vision, his choice of architects, and how it inspired her to be part of something larger against all odds:

I knew it was going to be very difficult, and I can remember our Ivy Plus group meeting in 1997. All of my facilities colleagues from the Ivies and Stanford were together at a meeting at Harvard at the time that Chuck's vision was emerging. It was very clear that this new building vision was going to happen; the only question was how big it was going to be. I can remember every one of my colleagues saying to me, "Vicky, you are never going to survive this, and you realize that, don't you?" I said to them, "Look, I have thought this through. I have been at MIT a very long time, and I love the institution, and an opportunity like this doesn't come around very often . . . and I am going to cast my lot with someone who has a vision and has articulated it so well." Why wouldn't I? Am I sorry? Absolutely not! So I came to think about Chuck as a leader in a very, very different way. To me, before this time he was an engineer, you know, a left-brain person, not very easy to talk with, and then as I worked with him I developed nothing but respect for him . . . I will never change my mind about my choice in following him.

When placed in the larger context of the major initiatives and decision-making patterns of President Vest, such as the OpenCourseWare project (OCW), standing up to the Department of Justice, the handling of the aftermath of student Scott Krueger's death, placing bets on the emergence of neuroscience as a major research area, and calling attention to the status of women faculty at MIT, what emerges is a leader who is transformational by any scholarly definition available. Anne Margulies, who led OCW under Vest, accentuates the president's impact on MIT (Karagianis, 2004):

> It absolutely wouldn't, couldn't have happened without Chuck Vest's leadership. He led the way in communicating the vision and got everyone behind it.

Further, Margulies notes how Vest recognized great ideas no matter where they arose in the organization (Walsh & Bowen, 2011):

> I don't think this ever would have happened at any place but MIT, or under any leadership but Chuck's. . . . Faculty come up with great ideas every day, but the leadership Chuck showed to seize this idea was really extraordinary. Though Vest and Brown have both left MIT, OCW continues to receive attention from administrators at the highest level. According to Lerman, "One of the virtues of Chuck Vest's unequivocal commitment was that it was passed on to future presidents and provosts," a legacy bolstered by the fact that Vest dedicated not only his presidency but the institution as a whole to establishing OCW as a permanent feature of the MIT academic program.

The Disruptive Charrette

In March 1999, President Vest, with a strong initiative by William Mitchell, convened a group of MIT leaders to brainstorm and envision the future direction of the organization (Mitchell, 1999), something that a routine or bureaucratically charged institutional planning practice could not accomplish.

Major architects were asked to be part of a design charrette[6] to envision the future of the MIT campus. Vest and his leadership team attended as did the major players of the planning and facilities team. The internationally prominent architects who were present included Charles Correa, Harry Ellenzweig, Frank Gehry, Steven Holl, Fumihiko Maki, and landscape architect Laurie Olin. The charrette was central to the identification of major issues and opportunities in shaping up Vassar Street as a major urban corridor, marked by the new campus housing on the west end of the corridor and the Stata Center as the northeast end. The charrette was influential in bringing the whole team of leaders and the then-prospective architects into one room and lighting a fire that would forge the projects. Vest noted the transformational nature of the charrette:

> So we really had a lot of engagement. . . . I did keep pushing on being aesthetically interesting, and then as you know, we did organize a two-to-three-day charrette where we got all the architects, and Laurie Olin came to think through the campus. I engaged in those things, but I am not reluctant to admit that I learned more than I provided. I had a feel

for it; I had a deep concern for it, and in the end though my strongest role was keeping this projects moving after the economy. That was very hard work.

Olin recalled the activities that took place over three days:

We thought about issues that had to do with how the campus might grow, but also things that bothered us, about the things at MIT that weren't the best version of themselves. And I pitched that, well, so many smart engineers, why weren't they doing smart things with their campus? They were still putting water in the pipe and wishing it to go away, when they are at the bottom of the hydrograph, and the river was flowing, and it didn't make any sense. And they weren't a very green campus in any way, and that they were sort of backwards in a series of environmental issues, which struck me as peculiar for a technocratic institution. So, I was just like, poke, poke, poke, and Frank was having fun, and Maki was being very reflective and thoughtful, and Correa was advocating for why aren't the students here and so on.

Olin, as a landscape architect, was concerned more about the overall structure of the campus, not just one building or two. He was concerned, as was Vest, with the state of the then "back side" of MIT along Vassar Street. Olin further recalled the detailed discussions about the deeply problematic issues surrounding the MIT campus:

So, none of us had contracts, except Frank. We had no stake in it, and we were all busy enough that we weren't looking for work. So that was clear. We weren't there on the make. They wanted us to talk to them straight, so we did. Chuck Vest made it very clear that he was interested in what we might think. He really wanted to know, what do you think of this place, and it really also was clearly the point where he was going to make only one or two more things, and that would be whatever happened might be his legacy. So he cared deeply that we try something. So I made a bunch of proposals about what—about water, some of which we actually were able to do with what would become the Stata Center, and some of which never happened. Correa and I really wanted to reorganize the athletic area and the student living. And we were intrigued by the notion of the Infinite Corridor and thought it's not infinite enough. Why isn't everything really connected, and why are you at this arbitrary, this funny nineteenth-century railroad, and it seems to be limiting you? You really can't go into the river, and you can't go left or right. . . . So the question of how would MIT grow when they are already in a dense area, with a lot of polluted industrial ends and high rent districts and a whole series of difficult planning and legal constraints on them.

In a complete confirmation of Vest's original observations about the rundown conditions of the MIT campus, Olin spoke passionately about how MIT stood the danger of losing its competitive edge if someone did not fix the mess:

I was very intrigued by it all, and Chuck Vest was Chuck, he wasn't Charles, he wasn't Mr. President, he was Chuck. He was clearly a hands-on engineer who didn't make a big point of it, but he let you know that he felt he wasn't deeply aesthetic in ways that he valued and would like to be, and he respected creative people, and he respected the arts, but he just wasn't one. And he wanted to know, he wanted good people to come and do things, and he realized that in the past, they had had some remarkable architectural adventures that at MIT in a couple of periods, but they hadn't really for a while.

MIT had built, but they had built in a mediocre way that was instrumental but wasn't inspiring. The campus accomplished their goals. Their scientists and their students were able to perform at a very high level and have a sense of community, and that was successful. But, you know the palm trees are swaying at Caltech, and here it is ten above in the slush and snow. And why would I want to be in a place that looks like hell when I could be somewhere nice. If I could be anywhere, why would I be in a place that looks like hell, and I said, ultimately it's going to hurt you, and recruiting is going to hurt you, and faculty is going to hurt you, the students' morale, the whole thing, you know. And the landscape isn't something that's an add-on or a decoration; it's the structure of the place. And it's what everybody shares, and everybody doesn't share a great lab, but everybody shares the mess in the street. So Chuck heard that, and he believed in it. So the charrette led to proposals for various projects and some infrastructure ideas. We got a call, and we were asked to come and do some framework planning for MIT.

Not everyone was pleased with the charrette or delighted by the outcomes, said Olin. By many accounts, some in the MIT planning office saw the process as a threat, as a judgment on what they had done or had not done, and they reluctantly participated in the process as MIT was hit with a slew of strong ideas, questions about the status quo, and a sense of urgency about comprehensively fixing the campus. Vest heard the message clearly.

According to Vest and others, MIT does not engage in strategic planning as a matter of conscious choice. Like other leading institutions that do not have strategic plans, MIT wants to maintain flexibility to respond to risks and dynamically arising opportunities to which individuals and units respond in a nimble fashion.[7] So, events such as the 1999 design charrette became points in the timeline where surprising and radical propositions emerged that unsettled the insiders who preferred planned and predictable courses of action. Thus, the charrette become an important point in the process of architectural as well as more comprehensive institutional change that Vest recognized, and behind which he threw his weight.

The Ray and Maria Stata Center

One of the first projects, and certainly the most controversial, strategic, and consequential, to take root under Vest's leadership was the Ray and Maria Stata Center. Although the project began well before the 1999 design charrette, the truly strategic nature of the project was realized only in the charrette. What had been set to become another academic building became a place for all of MIT, a place that extended the Infinite Corridor,[8] and an emblematic building for the future strategy of MIT.

Figure 6.4. Ray and Maria Stata Center. © 2014 Damianos Photography. Used with permission.

The Stata Center, as it is popularly called, was initially conceived as a replacement for Building 20 (the Radiation Laboratory), but not as a re-housing of what was housed by the original building. By any description, Building 20 had become virtually unlivable, full of toxic materials such as asbestos and a maze of unmanageable nooks and crannies. Rad Lab, as the building was called when it was established during World War II, was a place that witnessed historical developments in technology that contributed to the transformation of the United States. The three-floor structure was built in 1943 as a temporary space for wartime research, expected to be demolished at war's end. The building went on to live for fifty more years.

The Stata Center, consistent with other works by Gehry, is an uncon-ventional building that has been described as a "three-dimensional maze," a "fractal," a "continual brain game," and a "fun building for serious people." Made of stainless steel of different colors, bricks, steel, and concrete, the Stata Center deceptively breaks down the enormous space of nearly 430,000 square feet in its two towers and multiple frag-ments that tilt, project out into space, and lean into or away from each other. These fragments are skillfully crafted, designed with the aerospace industry's CAD/CAM systems, and constructed using technologies that pushed the boundaries of building construction at time it was built. In many ways, the Stata Center represents artistic, design, and technological innovations that advanced the knowledge of architecture.

As a result of the vision that emerged from the earlier brainstorming processes and the 1999 design charrette, the replacement for Building 20 was to become a consolidation of computer science and artificial intelli-gence units that had been housed in rented spaces tucked here and there around the campus. Further, with the Stata Center in place, the intersec-tion between Vassar Street and Main Street was envisioned as the "front door" to the campus on the northeast side.

Brown, then-dean of engineering, in 1996 quickly took the lead in the "client committee" for the Stata Center. He became the provost in 1998 and continued to lead the building project. He recalled the circumstances that led to Vest's choice of architect Frank Gehry (and consequently, the avant-garde aesthetic for Stata Center). Once the northeast corner of the campus had been identified as a major node in the urban network of MIT's campus, the need for a strong architectural statement was estab-lished. Brown described his role and how Vest delegated the project to him after the selection of the architect:

> Chuck's big input was picking the architects. . . . Chuck was a great defender of the project as it grew because it grew through the design stage. His passion for picking Frank was there, and his passion for architecture was there, but this was not his project.

Figure 6.5.   Stata Center, façade detail. © *2014 Damianos Photography. Used with permission.*

Figure 6.6.   Vassar Street view of three major new buildings, seen from Main Street. Stata Center to the left, Brain and Cognitive Sciences Buildings to the right, Simmons Hall at the far end of the street to the right. © *2014 Damianos Photography. Used with permission.*

Vest corroborated the hands-off role he played in the architectural projects beyond his high-level input and making the big decisions such as the selection of architects, "On the whole, I was not very hands-on (with) the actual accomplishments of the projects."

Robert Brown's Leadership Role

Vest let the notion that the building would act as a landmark in the northeast corner of the campus emerge from the design charrette. Much of the later considerations about the aesthetic characteristics of what was needed in that place were guided by the notion of an "iconic gateway" that emerged from that first intensive master planning session.

Given the centrality of the Stata Center, it is not surprising that the choice of its architect became very important. Vest described three elements that should guide the selection of architects for what would become the Stata Center: 1). Aesthetics that are in line with the identity of MIT, 2). What the building says about MIT, and 3). Accomplished at a reasonable cost. Of the three elements, the issue of cost was bound to remain more or less a constant given a certain profile of architects to consider. He recognized that just as an elite university costs more to attend, a high profile, internationally visible architect is expected to incur higher costs compared to any local and lower-profile architects. MIT trustee Raymond (Ray) Stata, an electrical engineer and 1957 graduate of MIT, was well known in the technology circles as the founding president of Analog Devices, a company based in the suburbs of Boston. He made his fortune with devices that act as bridges between the digital and analog signals in such products as cellular phones. The company posted revenue of $2.63 billion in 2012, and Stata served on the executive committee of MIT Corporation from 1984 to 2010. Ray and his wife Maria made a donation of $25 million in 1997 to jump-start construction of the gateway building.

In addition to the Statas, two other famous donors came forward to help fund the project. Bill Gates of Microsoft and Alexander Dreyfoos Jr. of Dreyfoos Group/Photo Electronics Corporation provided additional funding. As a result, the building named for the Statas had to be designed in such a way as to contain two towers, dedicated to each of the two other donors. Gates Tower and Dreyfoos Tower demonstrate how the shift from federal to philanthropic funding influenced architecture on campus.

Stata Center's floor area is over 430,000 square feet with a 290,000-square-foot underground parking garage. The building is significant for more than its gateway location and iconic design. It also serves as the loading and storage delivery area for the campus' underground tunnel system which moves goods between the laboratories and other buildings on campus. So, in many ways, the building is perhaps even more important, functionally and geographically, than Building 10, the famous Neoclassical dome building perched along the Charles River. The Stata Center occupies a strategic position on campus, says Brown:

> The concept of hiring Frank Gehry really came from the concept that this was going to be an iconic building on that corner of the property that became another gateway to MIT, and it works. You see in the literature, you see the dome, you see the Gehry building, maybe you'll see the dome twice as much as Gehry building, but people see the Gehry building, and they know that it is MIT.

By the time the Stata Center was completed, the role of the building on MIT's campus, the list of functions of the building, its tenants, client group, size, and cost, had evolved substantially. The building now houses Computer Science and Artificial Intelligence Laboratory as well as some of the denizens of Building 20, the Laboratory for Information and Decision Systems, and the departments of linguistics and philosophy. The building also has incorporated new functions that were hitherto not part of the demolished Building 20 or the northern part of the MIT campus.

Vest directed the building committee to produce three choices: one "high profile architect," one "really good architect" who had built on campus before, and one younger "up-and-coming architect." Vest summed up the challenge in front of him:

> I think that it is almost as simple as those who really wanted to take a risk and do something new versus those who did not want to take quite that large a risk. You know for most people, lay people, Frank was just coming into the fore. This was right after Bilbao was finished and so forth. And he had a reputation—right or wrong—for being expensive, for designing pretty complex structures that, to me, are not easy to take care off, so forth. So I think there was a little tension between are you willing to take a risk to do something right and important in the campus or shouldn't we?

There was substantial work done by the building committee which then consisted of William Dickson, the senior vice president; Allan Bufferd, the treasurer of MIT; Brown, the dean of School of Engineering; Sirianni, the director of facilities; and Mitchell, the dean of School of Architecture and Planning as well as the architectural advisor to the president. Later Lawrence Bacow would join the committee, and John Curry would replace William Dickson. The committee vetted a number of names of architects for Stata Center and shortlisted two. One was Frank Gehry, a controversial and exuberant designer, who employs cutting-edge digital technologies for design, making, and collaborating in the building process. The other was Harry Cobb from Pei Cobb and Freed, the firm founded by I. M. Pei, a famous alumnus of MIT who had completed several straightforward and noncontroversial projects on campus. By all available accounts, everyone involved in the architect selection process understood they had distinctly different choices at hand. One interviewee exclaimed, "Pei was a graduate of MIT. I do not think of his firm's buildings as being architecturally significant. Pei buildings are just Pei buildings." By all accounts, the final decision was Vest's.

The Blue Blazer

Vest has written and spoken much about the selection of Gehry. He says his decision was guided not by his personal preferences, but rather by his sense of what MIT needed at that specific time and on that specific site on campus. He said the following about his architecturally conservative personal preference versus what he thought MIT needed:

> I remember telling Frank (Gehry) one day after he started working I said, "Frank, you know what I personally like? What I really like is nice red brick Georgian architecture." That was what I always loved growing up and so on and so forth. That's not my responsibility here at MIT. That might be what I (personally) like. So, we had this great conversation in which Gehry pointed out that he always wears a Brooks Brothers blue blazer for the same reason.

The statement reveals Vest's sophistication and self-awareness with respect to institutional aesthetics of innovation, pushing boundaries, and taking risks. And the statement reveals his willingness to put aside his personal taste to make choices he thought MIT needed. He also distinguished how he chose different architects for different campus circumstances:

> When I visited campuses like Notre Dame, they were all very lovely but I didn't find them very interesting. I had no particular appeal of trying to somehow pull it back in a form that looked like MIT. The only place that we paid a lot of attention—and it wasn't me, it was the architects, and we were pretty clear with them—was really what became the Zesiger Center because that really was completing the plans that Saarinen had laid out, and we did not want to build the buildings that looked exactly like what Saarinen did sixty years before. We did have to make some sense out of that. I would not have wanted a Gehry-style facility there. We were very cautious about how that went. I think is a beautiful building. And the second thing is—I personally, or anybody else, didn't think that you wanted a huge number of Gehry kind of architecture—unusual buildings on the campus, but we needed some. We just needed more color and interest on the campus.

The notion of setting aside one's personal taste and preferences of architectural style is rare in academia where trustees, architects, building committees, and other leaders in charge of building projects are notorious to push their personal preferences over institutional needs[9] (Gunderson, 2000).

Vest met with both the firms that were shortlisted for Stata Center. He met with the building committee, which was split evenly between the two firms. He recognized that "the decision solely rested" with him (Mitchell, 2007). Vest sat down with Dickson, who led MIT's construction for four decades. In a moment of great consequence, Dickson made the following observation according to Vest:

> Well, let me tell you something. When our Chapel was designed by Eero Saarinen, it was considered so radical that the sponsoring foundation pulled its funding from it. Well, look how proud we are of it today.

In the end, Vest chose Gehry, and, as the expression goes, the rest is history. When Vest made the decision to choose Gehry, he knew he made a decision with tremendous consequences. A few evenings later, he told his wife Rebecca how he felt (Joyce & Gehry, 2004):

> I walked home and told my wife that I had just made a momentous decision, one for which I would be either admired or vilified in the future. MIT was going to take a huge step into a very different world of architecture.

In making the architectural choices, Vest and his team made repeated references to what MIT stood for, which was "Audacious innovation. It's about the future. MIT couldn't care a fig about the past." Vest made a case for the alignment between the choice of architects (and hence architectural characteristics), and the identity of the institution. For instance, he said in no uncertain terms what he intended for the Stata Center (Campbell, June 19, 2007):

> I believe that the buildings at this extraordinary university should be as diverse, forward thinking, and audacious as the community they serve. They should stand as a metaphor for the ingenuity at work inside them.

On another occasion, Vest reiterated his vision for the Stata Center. He said, "There is great variety and different kinds of adventure in what we do intellectually and educationally, and so it doesn't bother me at all to see that the buildings are taking that same approach. So that in the end, I think just kind of externally, they reflect a lot of excitement and the nature of what goes on at MIT."

In other words, Vest used the identity and values of MIT as driving criteria for making decisions as opposed to using his personal taste or the bottom line or the ease of maintenance or the ease of construction or any number of other criteria. Vest's team efforts were focused on how to elevate the experience of the physical campus to match or exceed the identity and stature of the institution. William Mitchell later reflected, "When colleges and universities build, they don't just add to their inventories of floor space. They reveal—sometimes unwittingly—their prevailing values, aspirations, and preoccupations" (Mitchell, 2007).

Brown recalled the moment of decision that was riddled with heated debates about the architectural choices recommended to Vest, debates that continue to be echoed today:

> (Vest) listened quietly to all the pros and cons. There were people on the program committee that absolutely did not want Frank because—and the truth is they were right—we spent money on community space and architecture that could have translated into more programs for them.

Simha, then-director of MIT's planning office, was also on the building committee and argued against the selection of Gehry (unless otherwise cited, material from the interview conducted with Simha at MIT on Sept. 12, 2012):

> I wouldn't say (Vest) certainly understood or appreciated the qualities of the best works that have been done at MIT, and I think he was, as most presidents do, trying to make this contribution in a way that was consistent with that. However he was persuaded by people who were very persuasive that MIT needed to build something like the Stata

building because "It would put MIT on the map"—and that's a quote. There were others who said, "MIT doesn't really need to be put on the map" through the device of architectural design, but that was one of the arguments that was used to justify Frank's building.

However, Vest felt that Gehry truly understood MIT and what the institute stood for. He felt comfortable and confident as he spoke to Gehry after the selection process (Joyce & Gehry, 2004):

It was clear that Frank Gehry already had a deep understanding of MIT and what we wanted to do. The fact is, we spent much of the time sharing tales about the late Caltech scientist Richard Feynman, an incredibly brilliant and colorful physicist who had been a student at MIT. Clearly, Gehry was an MIT person.

So, Vest knew what he would get by hiring Gehry: "I wanted to go with Frank Gehry, because we had to do something big, bold, exciting, and different to lead into the new century" (ibid.).

With One's Own Eyes

Decades before the Stata Center became the punching bag for critics, the MIT Chapel designed by Eero Saarinen had gained notoriety. A donor at that time threatened to pull out its philanthropic contribution to the project unless the architect was changed. Eventually, after understanding the project's architectural merits, the donor relented and supported the project. It was Stata Center's turn nearly five decades after the Chapel.

Vest led the way by engaging donors at the crucial time and convincing them of the appropriateness of the selection of the architect for the project. Alexander Dreyfoos, as one of the three major donors for the Stata Center project, was shocked, as were many in the MIT community, when he saw initial sketches and models of the project. Vest got the call from a deeply concerned Dreyfoos. What followed was characteristic of how Vest handled tough situations: by taking the high road and by placing trust in people that they would arrive at the right conclusion once provided with ways of understanding the situation. Vest recounted the process of convincing Dreyfoos:

The second major personal donor to Gehry's building called me one day after he had seen the drawings and was very unhappy—I mean REALLY unhappy. He said, "Chuck, what am I supposed to tell my friends? After spending all that money, and you are giving me this crushed beer can!" He said, "I am so mad that I am thinking about withdrawing my money."

Vest was in a bind also because Dreyfoos originally intended to donate his money to the Media Lab expansion project. But when the Stata Center became a priority, with the personal agreement of Nicholas Negroponte, then-director of the Media Lab, Vest convinced Dreyfoos to support the Stata Center instead.

> I felt I really owed him something. I said "Alex, I want you to do one thing. I will even buy the ticket for you. I want you to go out to Santa Monica. I want you to visit Frank's studio, and I want you to see the large-scale models that they have out there now." Well, Alex Dreyfoos made his fortune because he invented a lot of absolute top technology for films. He developed the machines that processed Kodachrome film. He has an Academy Award for Kodacolor. He is a great, magnificent photographer. So grumbling a little bit, Alex actually went out. And he had fixed his camera with a little fiber optic cable, a little fisheye lens at the end that he actually chained through the building, and (he) start taking pictures that showed what the thing would actually look like. Which as an architect you may look at and understand that; most of us don't. And he came back as an absolutely true believer. He showed me all these photos, saying, "Now I understand what this man is doing, and I think this is terrific!"

There were many grumblings and nasty emails that Vest received when people saw Gehry's early drawings and models. Vest tried to articulate how to understand the aesthetic of Gehry's architecture:

> Lot of people who were not central to the Stata Center would look at (Gehry's) drawings and send me nasty letters. A fairly common comment was—they would look at me kind of angry and say, "You think this is going to be a beautiful building?" I would say, "No, not in the sense that you mean beautiful. I think it's going to be really interesting. I think it is going to be, a kind of, representative of the audacity and excitement of people at MIT."

Ray Stata, the major donor for the building, was fully behind Vest's choice of Gehry:

> He had the courtesy of inviting me to his office and saying, "Hey, we've got a decision to make, and before I make it—he was clearly saying I have a decision to make—I want to have the benefit of your thinking about that." So, Vest said, "We've got this architect Frank Gehry who is kind of a wild man. And we also have a more traditional although clearly very imaginative architect in terms of Harry Cobb." And I think implied in there that there would be certain cost for someone not as traditional as Frank Gehry. And my response to that was, "MIT is a forward-looking institute; it's always looking to break new ground and have cutting edge representations of its mission." And therefore, the symbolism of Gehry's building—as he is reinventing architecture—would be clearly the most appropriate. And so, I had a no hesitation with that choice. That was great! That was exactly the conclusion Vest reached.

Stata's statement conveys that from a very early stage, Vest was fully aware that there would be a premium, in the form of additional cost and

Figure 6.7.   Stata Center. © *2014 Damianos Photography. Used with permission.*

controversy, to be paid with the choice of Gehry. This awareness counters some of the observations by critics who claim that Vest was naïve to not expect additional costs and managerial issues that go with the choice of star architects. For instance, Simha offered a critical observation that in his view, the financial burden had crossed a line at the institute, and the architecture was not driven by the budget:

> The procedure was to offer them a program and the budget, and the stipulation was that if they accepted the commission, they would agree that the design of the building had to be within 10 percent of that budget. If it exceeded that number at bid time, they were obligated to redesign the building until they brought the project into budget on alignment. During Chuck's time, that discipline was not maintained, and that had two effects. Obviously it appeared to give permission to do things which were perhaps interesting, but not necessarily consistent with the institute's resources, and it added substantially to the debt load that the president had to bear.

However, Executive Vice President Curry acknowledged that some people thought the projects were too expensive. He remembered different views of the future and different paradigms of fundamental values at play. Curry recounted a story about L.A.'s controversial Cathedral of Our Lady of the Angels:

> The architects Rafael Moneo and Buzz Yudell were meeting with Cardinal Mahoney about the cathedral, and the proposal was that it be built with reinforced concrete in earthquake territory. So the cardinal said, "I understand that it will withstand earthquakes, but over time what kind of problems might occur in this building?" Well, sometimes the concrete, for example, may become a little porous over many years. Water can seep inside, and sometimes the rebar rusts, but that is fifty years from now. The Cardinal said, "Well I just don't like that." And the architect said, "This is not going to be a problem for fifty to seventy years," and the cardinal said, "That is a big problem to me." So the architect asked him, "So how long do you expect this thing to last?" You know what his answer was? A minimum of five hundred years! In some sense, American campuses, the best campuses, have some of that character. They are here for years. Harvard is older than Boston. Harvard is older than America. Some of these campuses are long lived. While you don't want to make the buildings so unchangeable that they cannot be adapted, campuses are one of the few places where you can build for the ages and invest because when you amortize a building over a couple of hundred years, it doesn't seem as expensive as when you amortize in thirty.

Parallels to Vest's experiences could also be found going back to the 1950s when Eero Saarinen's design for Kresge Auditorium was called outrageous. A sponsoring foundation initially threatened to pull funding from the project but later relented. According to Sirianni, the building inspector of Cambridge at that time initially denied permits for Kresge Auditorium, citing the structure as unsound! Vest was aware of MIT's past engagement of controversial architects and avant-garde architecture and tried to draw from MIT's legacy of occasionally hiring high-profile architects who shook up the status quo on campus.

Curry remembered his conversation with Vest when he was hired as executive vice president. Curry's account further corroborates the fact that Vest was acutely aware of how he was returning to MIT's legacy of occasionally bringing highly prominent and avant-garde architects to build the campus:

> (Vest) said we are going to return to our occasional roots at MIT and seek innovative architects. He said we have a lot of building to do, and we are behind. We haven't built much in recent years. We have come out of the early 1990s recession, and it is going to be a very exciting time.

Furthermore, Curry observed the collaboration between Mitchell and Vest in reviving the debate about MIT's intermittent architectural risk-taking on campus:

> Between them, they revived the idea that MIT can do innovative architecture. I should mention the Saarinen buildings on the campus, an auditorium and a chapel. Those were outrageous for their times, so was the Alvar Aalto building, sometimes called the Pregnant Worm, along Memorial Drive. So if you walked that campus you saw risk taking, you saw Aalto who had not built anything except one building in this country. You saw Saarinen who was young who did the two pieces at MIT campus.

Brown corroborated Vest's observations about the appropriateness of choosing Gehry and noted that in the architect selection process, only Gehry addressed the issue of a gateway building effectively:

> Then there were other architects, some national, mainly regional, who did a lot more work, but you couldn't convince yourself . . . that they had done anything innovative about this gateway to that side of the campus. Some of them were more pedestrian: a firm did another kind of building in 1968 sort of double-loaded single-corridor thing that looked like traditional lab sort of buildings which you know, the campus is full of them so as to speak. There were a number of other architects with different kinds of designs like that, but no one really attacked the gateway problem.

The Stata Center swiftly went into design and construction. By all accounts available, faculty, students, and staff loved the project, and a majority of the building users continue to love the project. Brown reflected about the process and impact of the Stata Center: "What I first naively imagined to be the straightforward programming and design of an academic building evolved into a much more complicated journey that, in the end, challenged the very culture of MIT" (Joyce & Gehry, 2004). Brown further commented on how the Stata Center rivals the iconic status of Bosworth's buildings fronting the Charles River:

> What is remarkable is that the same MIT that holds commencement on the grand Killian Court surrounded by the Bosworth buildings can change our identity to embrace Frank Gehry's new vision of space for our academic community and its place in Cambridge and the world. Some will call the design eclectic. I think of it as a sign of the continual evolution and leadership of MIT. (Ibid.)

The process of design and construction of the Stata Center challenged assumptions held inside and outside MIT and pushed the boundaries of institutional architecture. One of those assumptions was the perpetuation of double-loaded corridors and pigeonholed laboratories where insular groups would be holed up for the rest of their lives. The Stata Center does not feature conventional corridors, conventional offices, and even conventional laboratories. There are no privileged horizontals or vertical levels in the building. Space is more volumetric with double or triple height volumes interconnecting multiple levels of work areas, allowing three-dimensional interactions. Conventional notions of hierarchy (that usually gets translated into hierarchical rooms, hallways, and configurations of center and margins) were turned upside down. In Gehry's words—consistent with the vision of Vest, and the observations of Brown, Terman, Mitchell, and others—the building is a balance between order and chaos. Gehry said, "I think of this in terms of controlled chaos. I always relate it to democracy. Democracy is pluralism, the collision of ideas" (Joyce & Gehry, 2004). He further articulated the guiding concept of design as follows:

> I am happy that this building expresses what's going on inside. My interpretation is that it reflects the different groups, the collision of ideas, the energy of people and ideas. They each have their own sorts of vectors and will all be colliding with each other, some accidentally, and some by contrivance. That's what will lead to the breakthroughs and the positive results. I think that's really going to work. I can't wait to see everybody in there, to see the beehive buzzing. (Ibid.)

The Stata Center did much to excite the stakeholders (or rile the opponents), motivate them, energize them, and provide tangible evidence that MIT was entering a new millennium with new energy. The project allowed the architect to apply his creative and technological ingenuity to engage MIT, and thus actualize the potential of both. The project allowed the client team, headed by Brown and Terman, to learn immensely about architectural processes, the larger purposes of architecture, and how to actualize their potential.

To summarize how the Stata Center touched even the most invisible and the least accounted-for stakeholders, the construction workers, Vest recited the story of how many of the workers actualized their potential through the project:

> There are lot of different stories, but one of my favorite things that I am going to tell you because I am never going to forget them is, when the Stata Center was two-thirds finished, I think most of the skin was going on, three or four of us toured the building for half a day with Frank while he was in town looking at everything, and we came walking through the basement. We were down in, probably, the first level of the parking structure, and this group of workmen recognized me and said, "Chuck"—they held me back and they said, "We just want you to know that every one of us left the jobs we were working on to come here and work on this project because everybody in town knows that something really important is happening here." I'll never forget that. These guys would bring their families over on the weekend. It really was kind of an event and a kind of venture that you'd like to have.

The Simmons Hall

At about the same time Gehry was hired in the fall 1997, the death of Scott Krueger galvanized Vest and others. A comprehensive and critical review—already underway when Krueger died—addressed the chasm between social opportunities, undergraduate student residential life, and the learning environment on campus. Vest set an aggressive schedule to build on-campus housing to accommodate all freshmen by the year 2000 as recommended by the Student Life and Learning Task Force.

In 1998, with the resignation of Provost Joel Moses, Vest set out to fill the position. Two candidates emerged in the search, and Vest liked both. Robert Brown was hired as provost, and Lawrence Bacow was appointed in the newly revived chancellor position. Bacow would oversee the new student initiatives and provide leadership for other student-oriented needs.

Bacow and the building committee led the charge to build the new residence hall. A number of local architects as well as national and European architects were considered. Of the five major buildings built under President Vest's tenure, Simmons Hall was the most contentious building when it came to the selection of the architect.

Mitchell advocated Indian architect Charles Correa—a 1955 graduate of MIT, and Portuguese architect Alvaro Siza with a hope of repeating the success of Finnish architect Alvar Aalto's famous design of Baker House. Bacow strongly disagreed. Given the project's aggressive schedule, he wanted to hire someone stateside. He reminded the committee of how much time Brown put into flying to Gehry's office in Santa Monica for the Stata Center project and noted that flying to Lisbon for design updates would be impractical. Steven Holl and William Rawn were also considered. Trustee Richard P. Simmons pledged $20 million toward the resi-

**Figure 6.8.   Simmons Hall. © 2014 Damianos Photography. Used with permis-
sion.**

dence hall, earning naming rights. Thus, Simmons Hall began to take
shape in a process that demonstrated that architectural and campus development is a process with multiple, multi-directional, messy, serendip-
itous, and surprising forces that reflect the organized chaos of a collegial
academic institution.

In the end, Vest and the committee agreed upon Steven Holl as the
architect for Simmons Hall. The development of Simmons Hall has been
well documented elsewhere (Gannon, 2004; Mitchell, 2007), but the leadership story of the institutional processes has not been adequately explored. Holl's design was part of a troika of residence halls along Vassar
Street. As it stands now, Simmons Hall is, thus, only one part of the
original vision that might not be completed in the near future.

The same criteria that applied to the selection of architect for Stata
Center were applied to Simmons Hall. Bacow recounted the notion that
MIT had not undertaken an architecturally significant initiative in its
housing projects in the fifty years since the opening of Alvar Aalto's
Baker House in 1948: "MIT housing with the exception of Baker House
had been pretty uninteresting, and housing traditionally in MIT had been
a refuge for students where they withdrew from the faculty."

Recalling the challenge of selecting an architect and then working
with the architect for Simmons Hall, Bacow said:

Steven Holl was poetic in his description of what should be done, and I think we were all taken and engaged by him. Working with him was a challenge, and the building that we built was the third or fourth design that we went through. He practically designed a complete building for us that we really liked, one with curved ramps, which we could not build because it wasn't fire code compliant. There was no way that the city would allow us to build it. That frustrated me enormously because we were so far behind schedule at that point. I just assumed an architect of Holl's stature would design something that could be built.

As it turned out, Simmons Hall proved to be the most difficult building to build due to its innovative structure and also the most expensive residential building per square foot of cost in MIT's history by all available accounts. According to Sirianni, the unit cost of Simmons was not higher than that of the Stata Center, but was very high for a housing project; in fact, it was the highest cost university housing project on the books at that time. Sirianni pointed out; however, that half the space in Simmons Hall was common space and not devoted to student beds and thus, it was an atypical housing project. The building also included a meditation space, following the needs outlined in the MIT Student Life and Learning Program. Holl's intentions were consistent with Vest's call for innovative architecture that pushed boundaries and took risks (Gannon, 2004):

> It has to be an inspired place for the students to live in a one-year, day-to-day existence at one of the most high-pressure universities in the country. One thing I think this building ought to do is distract them. It should playfully nudge them into thinking about something other than the problems with their studies. . . . I wanted to make a building that would not be taken for granted. It should engage its occupants, should become a part of their lives. Its calling is more than just the problem of a dormitory. . . . I am most concerned with that emotional and spiritual component that is never part of the program. That is the most difficult and most important part.

The difficulty of constructing Simmons Hall stemmed from the inventive new structural system, which is the building's outer envelope (wall and fenestration system) that was being done for the first time at such a large scale. The innovative structural facade gave a new meaning to the phrase "pushing the envelope." Vest's relationship to the Simmons Hall architect selection, design, and construction process was markedly different from that of Stata Center. Vest noted the effort it took to build Simmons Hall:

> Steven Holl's dormitory, which is a very interesting building, which by the way the students like—I go back and test the waters every now and then. That was a very difficult building to build, very difficult. You know it's interesting because people look at Frank Gehry's building and say, "Oh my gosh that must have been a tough one!" There were a couple of problems with Stata Center, but on the whole (Gehry) knew

Figure 6.9.   Simmons Hall viewed from Vassar Street. © 2014 Damianos Photography. Used with permission.

how to do these things by that point. Steven Holl's dorm, when you look at, it is all kinds of rectilinear things. Well, that's a piece of cake! But this thing is built out of precast concrete pieces. Every one of them is different, and it has to go up in just the right order maintaining the loads, and that building was really, really hard to build. My executive vice president (Curry) spent a lot of time. And I think the only reason that we got through it is that the president of the construction company (Daniel O'Connell Sons, Inc.) took a personal interest. I think he spent 50 percent of his time on-site for a couple of years. That one was hard, and so that's when we sweat up a lot, and of course we had to get up and be running by the time the school started. It had been set back by a year because of a nuisance suit from the person who owned the adjacent plot.

With the legal issues surrounding Scott Krueger's death mounting, and with an aggressive schedule for the residence hall announced, Vest delegated to Bacow the responsibility of leading the Simmons Hall project. Bacow, a lawyer by training and a professor of urban planning, was outside of the circle of administrators directly involved in the Krueger incident and thus also was tapped to guide MIT through the legal process. Essentially, Vest was required to keep some distance between him and the projects and processes concerning both the legal battles and the Simmons Hall project. Bacow noted:

> When I became chancellor, one of the first things that Chuck said was, "Larry, since you weren't in the administration at the time that Scott Krueger died and since you're also a lawyer, you're going to be our lead person in coordinating the institute's legal response to the district attorney's investigation."[10]

Furthermore, Brown noted that Simmons Hall would not have the same status as Stata Center in defining MIT. He summed up the entire process:

> Almost everybody was against picking Steven Holl because everyone knew that if he picked Steven Holl, Chuck was going to lose his date and that Holl couldn't design a building that fast. Steven Holl's firm was a tiny firm at that time. What was more important: bringing the students on campus by the date you set or getting an architecturally significant building. There were other people who had interviewed for it—good dormitory residential hall people—and Chuck picked Holl. Then Holl picked a design that was heck-harder-than-hell to build. The way it is cantilevered, the way the shell holds the way to the building, so the building ended up almost being two years late. It barely got open a year later. Vest took a lot of heat because of that. Larry Bacow who was chancellor at that time, took a lot of heat because of the lateness of the building. It is probably a more visible piece of architecture than Stata is to the rest of the city, but it is not iconic for the campus the same way Stata is because residence halls don't play that role.

In the end, Simmons Hall got built, the students moved in, and everyone on or off campus had an opinion about the building. Curry considered the tradeoff MIT made in taking on such bold and challenging projects as Stata and Simmons Hall:

> We have a real estate division at the treasurer's office. It manages Cambridge real estate, and it was pointed by too many that it's the way MIT ought to go. They built a graduate student dorm, a four-story brick building on the fringe of the campus. It was as dull as they'd get, but it functioned very well as a residence hall, and its house per square foot was a hell of a lot less than Steven Holl's building. There won't be a soul today to visit that building. In fifty years nobody will recognize that building as even remotely related to Massachusetts Institute of Technology. They'll still recognize Saarinen's Chapel. They'll recognize Steven Holl's building. They'll recognize Frank Gehry's building. They'll recognize Alvar Aalto's building, and the list goes on. And they will say that that was particularly MIT.

Simmons Hall tested not just a new architectural and structural problem, but it also tested the leadership nerve and perseverance and the institution's ability to raise resources for the ideals that it believed in.

The Appetite for Risk

Simmons Hall was an accomplishment that demonstrated Vest's willingness and that of his team to take risks and promote innovation even when they were under enormous pressures of time and resources, which could be read either as foolhardy or heroic depending on the perspective of the observer. What cannot be disputed is that the team realized one of the most complex and innovative structures of our time, one that is for the textbooks of history, structural engineering, and architecture.

During the 1990s and 2000s, Boston was besieged by mega construction projects such as the $16 billion Big Dig (an underground tunnel system to bury major transportation arteries in the city) and a $3 billion development of other major projects in the Boston Harbor area (Boston's big dig gets bigger, 2001; Diesenhouse, 2000). The cost of other major projects underway in the Boston area, such as architect Rafael Vinoly's Boston Convention Center, also went up by $100 million (Vennochi, 2001). Every construction worker and tradesperson was comfortably employed by the projects. The situation did not help MIT's building projects (or any other major building projects in the city) as it drove up the cost of labor and materials and made labor difficult to find. In some cases MIT received fewer than two bids for many of its subcontracts.

Curry spoke elaborately about the prudent and detailed financial modeling, reporting, and fiscal management measures during the turbulent economic times leading up to the turn of the millennium:

Figure 6.10.   Simmons Hall, corner entrance. © 2014 Damianos Photography.
Used with permission.

We had a ten-year financial plan with our board to spend "excess endowment earnings" of a specified amount from the prior decade to support early-year debt service on our capital projects—and no more. We pledged to balance operating budgets within that framework. We also understood that MIT's balance sheet was quite underleveraged and that we could add debt to a certain level without jeopardizing our bond rating. We updated the financial planning model virtually every two or three months to assess and report to the executive committee the consequences of our capital projects on all these constraints. If costs went up, what was the effect on debt? Our credit rating? Our ability to balance the operating budget? Same issues if fund raising was falling short. When the dot-com bust took our endowment down, we had to cut operating costs to offset the decline in endowment income to the operating budgets. But when endowment declines, the ratio of debt to financial assets goes up—affecting a key credit rating ratio. We modeled and reported the effect. When gift goals for a certain building began to fall short, we delayed start of construction. When we could see overly expensive characteristics of buildings, we redesigned.

Curry described how the construction projects responded to the financial modeling that ensured the risks were well within the parameters for MIT:

The modeling of our operating budgets and balance sheet together in real time, as changes from assumptions and projections occurred, provided a kind of continuous glue to keep this enormous initiative constrained. So while there were many moments of anxiety and push back, we and the trustees were always informed and not only accomplished a very aggressive and enlightened building program, but also kept within the key boundaries stated from the outset.

For Vest, it was important that the MIT community be able to look back at the architectural choices from a hundred years down the line and understand what MIT stood for: experimentation, risk taking, innovation, and boldness. The facts that the residence hall opened one year later than intended, and that its budget nearly doubled by the time it was completed, were likely to remain no more than footnotes in institutional memory. Mitchell characterized the tradeoffs between cost and risk and being faithful to the ideals and identity of MIT:

In a few years, the controversies will be forgotten, and an extraordinary architectural achievement will remain. It will continue to represent a passion for invention, a reproach to the practice of treating dormitory space as a standardized commodity that is planned by technicians with spreadsheets and ordered up like office supplies, and a refusal to reduce architecture to historicist branding that evokes some supposedly golden era of the past.

While Stata Center and Simmons Hall received immense press, design awards, and favorable as well as unfavorable attention, three other major projects and a number of smaller ones took shape under Vest's leadership, relatively quietly. Receiving universal praise were the Al and Barrie Zesiger Sports and Fitness Center designed by Sasaki with Kevin Roche playing a major design role, the MIT Media Lab expansion designed by Fumihiko Maki with Leers Weinzapfel, and the Brain and Cognitive Sciences Center designed by Charles Correa in partnership with Goody Clancy. Stata Center, while presenting some challenges in maintenance, is well-liked by users and by donors. Most important, MIT's academic departments say they have achieved greater distinction, gained a competitive edge, and enjoyed greater success in recruiting faculty members and graduate students in part due to the aesthetic attributes of the building and the risk-taking attitude they represent (Campbell, June 19, 2007).

As vice president for resource development during Vest's tenure, Barbara Stowe directed fundraising at MIT, running a successful $1.7 billion campaign. She articulated MITness in clearest terms: "MIT is less about sustaining and honoring tradition than it is about the future and the spirit of innovation, creativity and entrepreneurship" (MIT News Office, 2005). Senior Lecturer Chris Terman observed, "If I had to say you know, one sentence about how MIT is different, we're much more about making sure that the edges of the disciplines overlap." Simha expanded on the

Figure 6.11.   Stata Center, Vassar Street entrance. Brain and Cognitive Sciences Building could be seen across the street. © 2014 Damianos Photography. Used with permission.

notion of overlapping disciplines, tying those to the physical fabric of the campus:

> And those kinds of interactions are very, very powerful. Some of the most important scientific discoveries around here occurred as a result of people being able to move horizontally from mathematics to chemistry to physics to material science to electrical engineering and interacting with people along the way and having opportunities to talk about things or to enquire about things from colleagues and so that they never would have had if they existed in separate buildings.

Terman echoed Mitchell's observations about being consistent with institutional identity versus being driven solely by the bottom line, and characterized the tough leadership decisions taken by Vest as follows:

> As it turns out, despite howls of pain for a little while, MIT is actually doing fine. Certainly, Chuck must have done something right for us to have done well enough. It wasn't like we were a complete bankruptcy of some sort. . . . So in some sense, the decisions around this investment were not out of character for Chuck in the sense of thinking things through, and maybe ignoring advice from some quarters, and choosing a different path. He was showing his colors, in some respect but consistently with other things that he had done.

It is possible to pose questions about Simmons Hall from the perspective of innovation and risk. Even the most technologically advanced and managerially seasoned company such as Boeing has been set back by $4 billion cost overruns and long delays in the design, construction, and delivery of the Boeing 787 Dreamliner project, which suggests that innovation entails risk and uncertainty despite the best organizational efforts (Deckstein, March 30, 2011; Hiltzik, 2011).

The Rewards

Vest's presidency was one of the longest terms at any elite university in its league, and also one of the most consequential in terms of shaping an institute and the higher education world. Vest presided over what has been described as the third major building boom in MIT's history. Vest's choice of architects, in two of the five instances where he made the call, has been deemed controversial and risky. The Ray and Maria Stata Center designed by Frank O. Gehry and the Simmons Hall designed by Steven Holl have attracted the most attention, resources, and controversy mostly for the aesthetic choices. The five major works of architecture added 25 percent to the overall space of the MIT campus and reconfigured the academic landscape in substantial ways.

Financial risks and stewardship have been points of major criticism by a considerable number of critics within and outside of MIT. However, MIT has consistently maintained "Aaa" rating from Moody's and "AAA" rating from Standard & Poor's, a measure of MIT's financial stewardship and overall leadership (MIT News Office, 1996). The MIT endowment outperformed the S&P 500 consistently over the last decade or more (Hawkinson, McGraw-Herdeg, & Nelson, 2009). Most important, MIT's endowment under Vest's tenure grew from $1.4 billion to $5.1 billion, which created more resources for MIT than what was spent building up the campus.

At this point, one would be tempted to establish a causal relationship between large-scale campus building by hiring star architects to design marquee buildings and the institution's subsequent performance. While it is possible, it is difficult to verify such a linear relationship. Certainly there could be correlation between architectural excellence and institutional performance, but a causal relationship is much more challenging proposition, one that I do not feel needs to be made here. Moreover, architecture works on a grander time scale of centuries compared to any other institutional aesthetic intervention that could yield shorter term dividends. Creation of architectural work is an accomplishment in itself. Using architecture as a vehicle to accomplish other institutional goals is a second-level achievement that may take decades before its impact could be understood through qualitative or quantitative means.

The gray factory on the river was gone. It its place was a campus ready to tackle a new era.

NOTES

1. At MIT, the students and the hack became part of the cultural history of the institution that celebrates creativity and technical ingenuity with a sense of humor, hilarity and quirkiness (T. F. Peterson, 2011). At the Institute, hacks have a playful spirit and a positive fervor. Hacks are seen as demonstration of the creativity, technical ingenuity, and over the years, a variety of "non-destructive mischief went up on top of the iconic dome of Building 10: a fire truck, Pac-Man, an oversized gold medal, a lunar landing module, a police car, a small house, a smiley face, a giant snow man, and even a large "propeller beanie" (T. F. Peterson, 2011).

2. MIT does not have presidential terms. Once appointed, a president can continue in the position indefinitely.

3. The best available figure for the expenditures is $1 billion according to Mitchell (2007). The actual costs are not public knowledge, but some news sources put the cost of the various building projects during Vest's tenure at over $1.5 billion.

4. It is important to note that the decision to build Simmons Hall and move all freshmen to on-campus housing was announced in September 1998, two years before the settlement with the Kruegers took place (Sales, 1998). Scott Krueger's death sped up the process of change and accelerated the completion schedule for Simmons Hall. Contrary to the urban legend, Simmons Hall did not result from a settlement with the Kruegers. Although this alcohol-based tragedy accelerated Vest's decision and MIT's actions about student housing, there were many other fundamental reasons for it, especially the growing diversity of MIT students in every dimension. Multiple task forces had recommended making this change during the prior decade.

5. It is worth commenting, as a side note, that Campbell was in fact incorrect about Albert Einstein. Einstein wore his hair in a recognizable, radiant, and messy manner

that characterized his creative spirit and made him a visual icon that has come to represent scientific genius (Frederic Golden, 1999). Later in his article, Campbell acknowledges that the Stata Center does work. Campbell's description of the Stata Center is, by far, the most insightful and informative one despite its occasional slants.

6. A design charrette is an intense, limited-duration, collaborative design process in which people work together in a design studio in the early stages of a project to generate quick and multiple numbers of concepts and solutions.

7. Other prominent institutions that do not engage in strategic planning include Harvard University and Carnegie Mellon University.

8. Infinite Corridor is a quarter-kilometer-long hallway and an essential part of the MIT experience. The corridor acts as many things at once. It is a circulation spine that spans east and west through the buildings numbered 3, 4, 7, 8, and 10. Many labs, classrooms and departments radiate from the corridor. The corridor also acts as an iconic space through which the setting sun shines twice a year, which earned the corridor the nickname MIThenge.

9. In 1999, Lawrence Speck, dean of University of Texas at Austin's School of Architecture, resigned to protest how the architects Herzog and de Meuron were treated by the Board of Regents. The architects walked away from the $70 million Jack S. Blanton Museum of Art rather than compromise on the design. The UT Austin example shows how volatile decision making about campus architecture can be amid power struggles and imposition of personal preferences over promoting innovative architecture on campus.

10. The district attorney had impaneled a grand jury and named MIT as a potential target in the investigation of the death of Scott Krueger. The jury was ultimately dismissed without bringing any charges.

SEVEN

Analyzing Leadership Aesthetics at MIT

Fourteen years is a long time for presidency at any institution. It can be challenging to make sense of such long presidencies given their complexity and highly interwoven series of developments and connected people. Even when one looks at a thin, longitudinal slice of the presidency of Charles Vest, it is still a complex leadership phenomenon for sensemaking. In order to unpack and analyze the case, I will employ two lenses.

The first lens is aesthetics, consisting of four interrelated components:

1. The first component is the *architectural framework*, which provides an overarching taxonomy of three major aspects of leadership.
2. The second component is the *organizational aesthetics* framework, which provides an experiential basis to understand leadership in organizations.
3. The third component is the *organizational identity* framework, which connects aesthetic experiences with central character, distinctiveness, and temporal continuity of organizations.
4. The fourth component is the tacit *knowledge* framework (Polanyi, 1967; Polanyi & Grene, 1969), which links architecture as a body of experiential knowledge. The research questions reflect the focus on the intersection between leadership and organizational aesthetics as manifested in architecture.

The second lens is the *transformational and transactional leadership* framework (Burns, 1978a).

Vitruvian Triad and Leadership

Many of the previous commentaries on President Vest's leadership have been couched in terms of *utilitas* and *firmitas* (efficiency, cost, budgets, functionality, etc.) even when the critics' concerns were largely about *venustas* (the appearance and phenomenological aspects) of the buildings. Such criticism could be chalked up to the lack of sophisticated frameworks to understand aesthetic matters that belong to the realm of *tacit knowledge* (Polanyi, 1967) and how to relate aesthetics to organizational identity and mission, which belong to the realm of *explicit knowledge*. So, most commentators turn to easily accessible rational frameworks of cost, budgets, and quantity, and refer to familiar languages of architecture (styles such as Collegiate Gothic or simplistic categories such as beautiful or ugly) when confronted particularly by unconventional architecture.

Keeping in mind Pasquale Gagliardi's assertion that artifacts of an organization, such as architecture, not only represent deeper, underlying phenomena, but also are themselves primary cultural phenomena (Gagliardi, 1990; Strati, 2010). Further analysis shows the relationship between Vest's leadership and how he saw the cultural role played by architecture in the organizational setting of MIT shaping, challenging, representing, and promoting institutional mission, identity, and values.

Feeling MIT

Aesthetics embraces and recognizes the importance of visceral, bodily feelings and sensory experiences, not just thoughts and other cognitive processes. One of the findings of this study is that the president began his journey into MIT's aesthetic world early when he arrived freshly on campus, and those early feelings played a role in motivating the campus transformations that followed. He described his *feelings* toward the campus' physical environment, particularly the northeastern side of the campus, in no uncertain terms. He felt MIT looked more like a naval base than a campus for an academic community. He "confessed to a depressed feeling upon driving down the tired, treeless Vassar Street . . . decaying buildings, and nearly dilapidated and dismal gray-shingled Building 20 . . . " (Joyce & Gehry, 2004). Further, he recalled his "shock" at the sight of "dark space, run-down buildings, fifty-year old asbestos shingles, and chain link fences" on the backside of the "battleship gray" MIT campus (Vest, 2007).

Vest was not the only one who felt shortchanged by the campus conditions. Mitchell characterized the MIT campus of the 1990s as "grim and run-down" (Mitchell, 2007). Trustee Ray Stata called it "dreadful and very dreary." Terman corroborated that with his own complaints: "utilitarian, gritty architecture, poured concrete, rotten wood, and a warehouse-y little industrial company." Curry spoke about "the battleship gray MIT and the gritty dirty sidewalks." Clearly, there were no feelings of love for the rundown character of the MIT campus in those days. Most observers sensed a chasm between the world-class stature of the institute and the aesthetically deplorable conditions on campus. The repulsive feelings, as data suggest, created a strong emotional impetus for Vest and his team and motivated them to act.

Vest connected his feelings with those on campus to create a synergy with the opportunities that arose and forged a strategy that coupled resources and organizational change with the expansion and transformation of the Gray Factory on the Charles. Vest's case shows the strong role that aesthetic experiences and feelings can play in organizations.

Researchers have noted how architecture has been used to not only aestheticize organizations but also an-aestheticize people from feeling anything significant (Dale & Burrell, 2003). Particularly for those who have been at MIT for a long time, the Gray Factory was taken for granted, or they were resigned to the conditions. Vest's experiences upon his fresh arrival on campus provided the impetus necessary for the key constituents to take notice and bring about substantial architectural change.

Interestingly, Burns, when he discussed the life of Mahatma Gandhi, centered his analysis on how Gandhi felt on different key occasions such as the time he stole and confessed about it to his father; the time when he stepped aside from tending to his ailing father, the time he climbed into the "marital bed" only to receive the sudden news that his father had died in the next room, and the time Gandhi was ejected from a train for refusing to vacate his first-class seat in South Africa. The Oedipal and guilt feelings, Burns observed, shaped Gandhi in substantial ways. From these feelings, Gandhi drew motivation to sublimate his feelings, revolt nonviolently, and find a higher and moral expression in the way he led millions of people to their freedom (Burns, 1978a). In the case of Vest, the intersection between Burns's transformational leadership elements and aesthetic experiences led to substantial action. Unless the president "felt" strongly, and had the ability to rally people behind a common purpose, the transformation of the physical plant could not have come about the way it did.

The analysis reveals that the role and power of non-rational factors such as aesthetic sensibilities and visceral feelings in the decision-making process cannot be overestimated. Leadership and decision-making are often guided by rational and cognitive processes, but Vest's case shows that the non-rational approaches are often more important considerations that address the unconscious processes of individuals and institutions.

Fostering Shared Sense of Aesthetic

Vest fostered a shared sense of aesthetic that motivated, inspired, and drove the complex and multifaceted effort to transform the campus. College and university campuses are known by their bucolic and unified architectural styles or by a set of closely related architectural styles. Oxford University, Harvard University, University of Virginia, and many other institutions instantaneously call to mind coherent campuses of traditional buildings, often in brick or stone, interconnected by landscape. MIT is an exception to the general rule. Although William Welles Bosworth designed the Cambridge campus of MIT in Neo-classical style in contradistinction to a Jeffersonian academic village (Mitchell, 2007), the rest of the campus grew with no privileged architectural style, which has been a reflection of MIT's academic diversity and its relentless focus on the future. Aided by Mitchell's progressive views, Vest understood that the MITness of MIT did not lie in a unified architectural style but in the unifying themes of innovation and risk-taking that underlie the physical campus. His choices reflected his own interpretation of MITness, and his leadership advanced those ideals.

All the interviewees, donors, and Vest's critics in the public media have understood Vest's message about the fundamental criteria, whether they agreed or disagreed with the criteria, for architect selection and the kind of architectural characteristics that he envisioned. Innovation, risk-taking, boldness, audacity, pushing the envelope, and architectural significance have been the criteria that virtually all the interviewees and other constituents mentioned in interviews. Zeal similar to that witnessed among Apple fans could be seen in Vest's team and moving other stakeholders at MIT.

So, why was the shared sense of aesthetic qualities (not styles) important to Vest? And what was the opposition from those who disagreed with Vest's shared vision? Vest spoke about the qualities that should be embodied in MIT's architecture, such as innovation, boldness, risk-taking, and creativity. He did not speak about what styles MIT should adopt. Further, he did not advocate for one architect to design multiple buildings in one style. On the contrary, he said, "I personally, or anybody else, didn't think that you wanted a huge number of Gehry kind of architecture—unusual buildings on the campus, but we needed some."

Vest focused more on MIT's underlying values and qualities and sensed the particular needs of each of the sites for the new buildings on campus, which allowed him to take the discourse about architecture to a deeper level and to deeper themes. Focusing on deeper institutional themes relates to Burns's (1978) notion of a transformational leader who "makes conscious what lies unconscious." Vest's sense of aesthetic went deeper than the veneers of buildings and their stylistic characteristics, which is a feat that even trained architects can find challenging. Vest's sense of aesthetic was closely tied to and guided by his focus on MIT's mission and evolving (and conflicting) identity.

Aesthetics as (Expression of) Mission

President Vest made an effort to connect the institutional mission, values, and identity of MIT with architectural experiences. Following the Vitruvian triad, mission of an institution describes the utility and reason for existence of an organization (*utilitas*). The mission (*utilitas*), physical plant (*firmitas*), and the sensory experiences or vision (*venustas*) of an institution must be aligned for the institution to *deliver* on its mission. The mission is manifested, expressed, and concretized in some kind of physical form—architecture, visual graphics, specific sounds—that is experienced by people through their sensory encounters. Mission is articulated in words, thoughts, and *explicit* knowledge, whereas sensory experiences are felt in the *tacit* realm as feelings and *experiential* knowledge. There are two levels at which MIT's aesthetics and mission were connected and given expression through Vest's leadership:

1. Phenomenal and aesthetic level (Gagliardi, 1990; Polanyi, 1967; Strati, 1999a): MIT's mission of knowledge creation was advanced by the creation of *tacit knowledge* in the form of sensory and visceral experiences through architecture
2. Cognitive and symbolic level (Jencks, 1991): MIT's identity, culture, and values have been "represented," "communicated," and "articulated" using architecture as *explicit knowledge* and language.

The first level is that which Gagliardi refers to as "artifacts as primary cultural phenomena" (Gagliardi, 1990) in contradistinction to Schein's notion that artifacts only act as referents to underlying organizational values (Schein, 1992). Here, Gagliardi is referring to the status of artifacts as bodies of tacit knowledge. The focus of this analysis is on the first level concerning aesthetics.

Vest and his team understood that the architecture of an institution is tacit knowledge produced by the institution. MIT's fundamental mission is to create and advance new knowledge. However, "knowledge" is usually interpreted, in a limited sense, to be explicit knowledge in the form of *scholarship of discovery*, to borrow from Ernest Boyer's fourfold classification that also consists of other forms of explicit knowledge such as *scholarship of integration, scholarship of application*, and *scholarship of teaching* (Boyer, 1994).

The notion of tacit knowledge is important to understand the phenomena of organizational aesthetics (Gagliardi, 1990; Strati, 2010). As discussed earlier, tacit knowledge is the knowledge that one possesses but cannot necessarily articulate ("We know more than we can tell"), and from which emanates *explicit knowledge* (Polanyi, 1967). Aesthetic experiences largely belong to the realm of tacit knowledge for most individuals who are not specifically trained to translate them into explicit knowledge.

Vest intuitively understood and advanced MIT's mission of knowledge creation into the realm of tacit knowledge by leveraging the physical plant. For instance, as previously mentioned, he spoke of how he negatively felt, experienced, and was moved by the dull, dreary, dark, and dreadful state of MIT's physical plant. He spoke elaborately about MIT's past efforts at tacit knowledge creation through the works of Eero Saarinen, Alvar Aalto, I. M. Pei, and other architects. Vest then felt the need for "color, excitement, and openness," all of which are experiential terms. He also spoke of the need for MIT to not just be a world-class university, but also for the campus to feel world class. Vest's intuitive sense of MIT's need for color, excitement, and openness reveals his intentionality in the context of the "Gray Factory."

Mitchell, Vest's architectural advisor, acted as the spokesperson for Vest's leadership team regarding its architectural undertakings. He summarized the administration's moral stance about the creation of tacit knowledge: "It is a fundamental responsibility of universities to pursue architecture and urbanism at the highest intellectual level and the highest level of cultural ambition" (Biemiller, Jan. 28, 2008). Furthermore, the knowledge-creation mission of MIT was very much on the mind of the leadership team: "We have the world's most important work to do, the creation of knowledge and the sharing of wisdom, and we bring to this work exemplary values. . . . We need architecture in which to do this work and with which to express these ideals" (Biemiller, Jan. 28, 2008).

Both Vest and Mitchell point to the double standards of some in academia in which the same standards of expectations from scientific research are not applied to the architecture of the institutions. For instance, Mitchell pointed out that universities are happy to settle for "mindless commodity architecture" but not for "second-rate physics or banal history" (ibid.). The transformative power of architectural change was confirmed by how the altered "feel of MIT experience" provoked fierce opposition that Vest received from all quarters, particularly at the beginning stages of the Stata Center, and continuously from external critics who might not be aware of the deeper dynamics of tacit knowledge at the institute and the changing identity of MIT, or who might be speaking from the viewpoint of their respective institutions (Campbell, June 19, 2007; Chamberlain, 2004; Silber, 2007).

The second level where evidence suggests that Vest connected MIT's mission, identity, and values with aesthetics relates to Edgar Schein's notion that architecture reflects underlying assumptions and values (Schein, 1992). Vest, on many occasions, articulated the expressive potential of architecture and how architecture should express the "audaciousness, boldness, excellence, innovation, creativity, risk-taking, experimental spirit, brilliance, and excitement" of MIT. With conviction about the expressive potential of architecture, Vest clearly expected the built environment to capture, express, and tacitly or explicitly communicate the essence of MIT from the turn of the millennium and to posterity.

The impact of architectural changes is not just experiential (*venustas*), but also proved to be lucrative (*utilitas*). Recent developments confirm that, at a strategic level, MIT had turned a corner due to the changes to the physical plant, which opened up new opportunities and new partnerships and singlehandedly shifted the center of MIT from Killian Court and Building 10 to the new epicenter anchored by the Stata Center and the Brain and Cognitive Sciences building. Recent reports indicate that, in great part, MIT's campus development strategy under Vest has yielded rich dividends to the tune of $2 billion by attracting a range of corporations that moved into the neighborhood to partner with MIT (Cohan, 2013).

Vest's case shows the dynamics between MIT's mission (*utilitas*), the physical artifacts of the institution such as architecture (*firmitas*), and the vision (*venustas*). Often, such dynamics take place at a subconscious level of an institution. In Vest's case, there is an unusual level of awareness of the need for close alignment between the three realms, and yet the alignment was not reduced to a shallow enforcement of a veneer-based aesthetic decision (such as all-brick or all-stone building skins that could be found on many campuses). While mission is about what an institution does (*utilitas*), identity is about what an institution is (or wants to be), which raises a different set of questions addressed in the following section.

Aesthetics as Expression of Institutional Identity

A key finding in Vest's case is that, in making architectural choices, Vest and his team connected MIT's identity and the choice of architecture. Vest's team efforts were focused on how to "elevate" the experience of the physical campus to match the changing identity and international stature of the institution. Although all the major institutional decisions are "approved" by presidents, it is exceedingly rare for a president of an institution to be directly involved in making intentional architectural choices in an effort to make sense of institutional mission and identity and to express the institutional values in the enduring medium of architecture.

Vest was aware that MIT has always oscillated between utilitarian and normative identities. Maclaurin's technology plan of 1919 took MIT closer to tightly coupled industry partnerships in an effort to raise funds, which pushed the Institute to adopt a more utilitarian role that belied the construction of MIT's stately new campus designed by Bosworth.

By 1930s, under Karl Compton, MIT turned the corner from being a polytechnic institute (utilitarian) to that of a research university (normative). During the 1960s, MIT debated and questioned whether classified federal research belonged on campus (Kaiser, 2010). As a result of the evolution of identity, MIT shaped into a normative institution that transcended its original utilitarian origins. However, the tension between the utilitarian and normative roles and between the science and engineering dimensions continues to fuel the periodic debates at the institute, which invariably bubbled up during Charles Vest's presidency and influenced architectural changes.

An institutional effort to promote architectural excellence on campus and portray architectural leadership could be traced as far back as the early 1900s when Welles Bosworth designed MIT's Cambridge campus on the Charles River. Those early efforts were followed when Alvar Aalto designed the Baker House dormitory in the 1940s, followed by Eero Saarinen's works built in the late 1950s, and I. M. Pei's tower built in the 1960s. However, the earlier interventions were interrupted by a long pause until the late 1990s and early 2000s.

President Vest was well aware of the long pauses after the 1940s and 1960s and noted that although some architecturally interesting structures had been built on campus, there had not been an intentional and concerted effort to transform the overall character of the campus from the gray factory for equipment to a humanized place for people. Nor had there been an effort to change from relying predominantly on the federal government (which earned MIT the reputation of being part of the military-industrial complex) to a more independent institution where humanities and creative disciplines flourished and federal, corporate, and philanthropic sources of revenue intermingled.

Vest understood the deep-seated desire of the institution to shed its utilitarian baggage. Vest and his team led MIT toward a strongly normative identity and aesthetic excellence. He and his team became the midwives of MIT's push for a more normative identity as it entered the new millennium. Burns's notion that a transformational leader makes conscious what lies unconscious is evident in the way Vest and his team resolved the competing identities of the institution through architecture by choosing what Dale and Burrell (2009) called "art-architecture" over utilitarian architecture, and by celebrating creative people and color over mere equipment sitting in a gray atmosphere. Architecture became a strategic tool to shift MIT's identity from utilitarian to normative self. The team accomplished this shift by employing a range of aesthetic categories other than just "beauty." The importance of understanding and applying a wide range of aesthetic categories is a skill that could empower presidents and institutions as it did at MIT.

The Beautiful, the Tragic, the Comic, and the Sublime at MIT

Architectural experiences are tacit knowledge for most people. They can "feel" more than they can tell. Certain architectural environments may feel familiar or strange, and yet one cannot tell why. In most cases, people use only one category of aesthetics—beauty—to understand and judge architectural experiences. However, there are other aesthetic categories that are essential to distinguish between different kinds of experiences such as *the ugly, the sublime, the gracious, the grotesque, the tragic, the picturesque, the comic,* and *the holy* (Strati, 2010). The extended range of aesthetic categories helps us appreciate, analyze and understand the nuances of aesthetic experiences offered by art, architecture, sculpture, music, theater, and dance.

At MIT, the beautiful, the tragic, the comic, and the sublime were strung together as experiences that, perhaps, only architecture could resolve in one stroke and as an enduring knot in time and space. Vest and his team sublimated the *tragic* circumstance of the death of student Scott Krueger into a *beautiful* experience at the Simmons Hall and the demise of the historic Building 20 (Rad Lab) into a *sublime* experience at the Stata Center, both of which were charged with humanizing and supporting student life on campus and blending academic and residential spheres of MIT into a flowing and unified experience.

The Al and Barrie Zesiger Center, which has been widely described as a *gracious* addition to the campus and a subtle architectural response to Eero Saarinen's Kresge Auditorium, plays a major role in orchestrating a *beautiful* experience.

Vest understood the sublime more than some gave him credit. For instance, Vest distinguished beautiful from sublime, calling the latter "interesting":

> Lot of people who were not central to the Stata Center would look at (Gehry's) drawings and send me a nasty letters. A fairly common comment was—they would look at me kind of angry and say, "You think this is going to be a beautiful building?" I would say, "No, not in the sense that you mean beautiful, I think it's going to be really interesting. I think it is going to represent the audacity and excitement of people at MIT."

MIT is a *sublime* institution. In popular culture, MIT is often described with nothing less than a sense of awe. Countless films and works of fiction have portrayed MIT as the place for geniuses, intellectuals, superheroes, creative individuals, innovators, entrepreneurs, and leaders who are held as paragons (*MIT in Popular Culture*, n.d.). MIT is, thus, not described as *beautiful* as much as it is described as *sublime*. Vest's intuitive as well as conscious effort to establish a correspondence between the identity of MIT as a sublime institution and MIT's physical plant as a sublime experience epitomized by the Stata Center would make sense when seen through the aesthetic lens of *sublimity*. However, critics inside and outside of MIT have brought to bear utilitarian categories (*utilitas*) of cost, usability, efficiency, and functionality to explain their feelings about the architectural changes heralded by President Vest and his team.

Vest and his team could have used more sophisticated language to describe and make sense of the utterly strange forms, spaces, colors, and new sensibility. When people tried to put the square peg of a building in the round hole of the only aesthetic category they knew, the *beautiful*, the results were ugly vitriol.

The sublime is a category that aptly connects MIT and its newfound architectural expression in the Stata Center.

The Great Breast and the Great Hack: Shifting the Center

The Stata Center played an emblematic role in the entire campus transformation under President Vest. It is possible to explain why it became the focal point of Vest's efforts to transform the experience of MIT as well as shift the center away from Welles Bosworth's Building 10 (the domed building).

Visually, viscerally, geometrically, and functionally, Stata Center has shifted the fulcrum of MIT's campus and MIT's strategy for the future away from Bosworth's complex. Stata Center has displaced the great dome of MIT as the epicenter of MIT. An aesthetic analysis of the dynamic tension between Building 10 with its great dome and the Stata Center reveals an underlying shift at MIT between the 1990s and the 2000s.

William Welles Bosworth's design for the Cambridge campus was built in 1916. The domed building, Building 10, is perched along the Charles River, stretches its "two arms" toward the river as if to invite Boston into its fold. The great dome can be read, phenomenally, as a nuclear reactor, as an echo of the great dome of Pantheon in Rome, and, as some hackers interpreted in 1979, as a "giant breast of knowledge" that nourishes the community (T. Peterson, 2003). Yet another possible interpretation of the dome is to read it as a Buddhist *sthoopa*, a cosmogonic egg that contains the relics of wisdom (Fussman, 1986). By its dynamic, hemispherical, geometrically pure form, the dome had become the iconic symbol of MIT from the early 1900s until the late 1990s.

Vest *felt* that neither the gray neoclassical buildings of the Killian Court complex nor the gray-brown brutalist buildings of the 1960s accurately reflected the new spirit of MIT and the emerging directions that took the institution away from predominantly federal dependency to a more diversified portfolio of revenues. Prior to Vest, buildings were seen as "equipment space" in which humans also got along. But, as described earlier, Vest wanted to soften and humanize the campus and make it livable for a broader cross section of users. Stata Center symbolized not just what it housed, but also a massive shift at MIT from the "dull, federal

Figure 7.1.   The Great Dome with "Fire Truck" Hack. Photo: Sarah Jane, public domain, CC 3.0, Wikimedia.

gray factory" of the past to a "colorful, playful, and exuberant" place for audacious, innovative, risk-taking, and creative individuals, a place that reflects the sensible foolishness (March, 1981) that is an integral part of MIT's identity.

Figure 7.2. The Great Dome and the Stata Center. Photo: DrKenneth, public domain, CC 3.0, Wikimedia.

Vest and Gehry envisaged the Stata Center as the new "gateway" to MIT, anchoring the northeast corner, and marking it in no uncertain terms. By placing the Stata Center right across from the Brain and Cognitive Sciences building (which architect Charles Correa imagined to be a precise building), Vest and his architects set up a contrast that steals the show on campus.

The Bosworth complex could be described, aesthetically, as hard, gray, sardonic, and potent (Figure 7.3). In contradistinction, the Stata Center is, as Frank Gehry described, a "playful building for serious people," a mix of the sublime and the comic. It is the building that reflects, as James March would say, the institute's *organizational foolishness* and its creative verve. Stata Center breaks down the gigantic scale of the amount of floor space it houses into discrete volumes that stand, tilt, nose, dance, reach out, fold, and act like a stage set on which unfolds the great drama of a great institution. While Building 10 speaks of singularity, the Stata Center speaks of multiplicity. If Building 10 is a tuxedo, the Stata Center is jeans and T-shirt. Building 10's *stateliness* stands in diametrical contrast to the "controlled chaos" and *geekiness* of the Stata Center.

By housing the two kinds of knowledge areas with the most future potential (artificial intelligence and brain sciences) together in the north-

Figure 7.3.   MIT Building 10, column detail. © 2014 Damianos Photography.
Used with permission.

east corner, Vest and his team left room to grow spatially and establish partnerships with a range of corporations that moved into MIT's neighborhood on the northeast side. Thus, symbolically, experientially, economically, and spatially, the Stata Center marks the future of MIT, its evolving identity, and its unmistakably normative status expressed and ingrained in the space and experience.

The dialogical relationship and the stark contrast between the aesthetics of the neoclassical and hemispherical dome and the fragmented deconstructivist towers of the Stata Center externalize the unconscious desires and identity struggles. One way the long-standing desire to subvert or at least bring levity to the neoclassical dome was through the hacks of MIT students. At the institute, hacks have a playful and positive fervor. As noted in the case, hacks are seen as demonstrations of creativity and technical ingenuity. Over the years, the dome was topped by: a fire truck, Pac-Man, an oversized gold medal, a lunar landing module, a police car, a small house, a smiley face, a giant snowman, and even a large "propeller beanie" (T. F. Peterson, 2011). In that sense, the "geeky" Stata Center could also be read, in the context of MIT's traditions, as an ingenious and permanent hack on the campus in the best tradition of MIT, employing cutting-edge technology and celebrating the playful, creative spirit of MIT's stakeholders.

Although there is no evidence that Vest and his team bore in mind the tradition of hacking while thinking about the Stata Center, as architectural theorist Charles Jencks (1991) noted about the communication potential of architecture, buildings are multivalent, which means they bear many levels of meaning, whether intended or not.

In sum, Vest and his team, in effect, established a tacit dialogue between the stately Building 10 and the playful Building 32—the Stata Center—as a way of shifting the fulcrum of activity to the northeast side of the campus, thereby signaling a change in the strategy and opening up new avenues, new combinations of disciplines, new partnerships with industry, and a new set of experiences as MIT turned the new millennium.

Transformational and Transactional Leadership

As noted earlier, Burns's framework could be summed up using six elements as discussed earlier: engagement, leader making, morality, motivation, making conscious what lies unconscious, and self-actualization.

Engagement

Burns distinguishes transforming leadership from transactional leadership with the concept of engagement. *Engagement*, as Burns defined it, stands in contradistinction to *exchange*. Leadership is a relationship that, when it engages the leader and the led, rises above the mundane, day-to-day exchanges, trades, political maneuvers, and transactions that are merely focused on the immediate task or project. Engagement conjoins the leader and the led with a *common and higher purpose*. One of the manifestations of engagement, for Burns, is when the leader not only teaches the led, but also is open to and is taught by the led, thereby enriching both. *Engagement* demands active listening.

Vest has been widely recognized for his listening skills. Every interviewee confirmed that Vest listened carefully to everyone and to all sides. Vest's engagement of his team comes from a combination of deeply respectful relationships and the ability to listen and be educated. For instance, Vest spoke about how he engaged, and was in turn taught by, Mitchell:

> I did actually appoint Bill Mitchell as the architectural advisor to the president, which was an appointment that had been made a few times in the past. So Bill played a very direct role, and all this was for me as much a learning experience as it was a leadership experience. Bill had a big impact on this, but he did so as a teacher.

Curry noted the engagement between Mitchell and Vest, who partnered to push the idea of innovative architecture at MIT: "Bill and Chuck had clearly hit it off well. . . . Between them, they revived the idea that MIT can do innovative architecture."

Vest reflected about his experience at the 1999 design charrette in which he noted how he contributed as well as learned from the experiences: "So we really had a lot of engagement. . . . I did keep pushing on being aesthetically interesting and . . . I engaged in those things, but I am not reluctant to admit that I learned more than I provided."

Olin corroborated Vest's reflection: "Chuck Vest made it very clear that he was interested in what we might think. He really wanted to know." He noted further, "Chuck was a man who had a vision, he was genuine, he was generous, he listened to people, he would engage you, he was happy if you would argue."

Burns's notion of engagement hinges on the importance of leaders and followers having a common and higher purpose that helps them be engaged and transcend day-to-day transactions. The theme of Vest's ability to engage people via a larger, higher, nobler, and common purpose repeatedly came up in the interviews and other sources of data. Bacow noted:

> The people who sat around that table at Academic Council were the most talented group of people I have ever worked with, just extraordinary people on both the academic and the administrative side. And [Vest] had a way of inspiring people and laying out broad brushstrokes of what he wanted to do.

Speaking of Vest's ability to frame a common purpose, Sirianni said, "I am going to cast my lot with someone who has a vision and has articulated it so well." Chris Terman also corroborated the notion of Vest articulating a common purpose that engaged him: "Chuck could obviously really connect with people. Chuck, I think, really worked on articulating missions."

Vest is a leader who could engage a wide range of people, listen to them, be willing to be taught by them, and communicate a vision that inspired them to do their best work. The two-way interaction and the bidirectional influence is, for Burns, one of the most important aspects of engagement. In Vest's case, the bidirectional influence meant that his team and other stakeholders felt they were deeply respected, inspired by common purpose, and meaningfully engaged, which ultimately led to their elevation to a higher level of morality.

Leader Making and Team Building

Vest carefully and intentionally chose his subordinates, entrusted them with major responsibilities, and guided and mentored them in ways that helped team members find their full potential and actualize their potential, which could be described as the educational process at its best. The example resonates with Burns's notion that transformational leaders inspire the led to become leaders in their own right.

Bacow, for example, said: "We all watched what Chuck did. He was very forthcoming with advice. He was very supportive of each one of us when we were thinking about leaving. I mean, no holding back or anything else like that, very, very supportive."

Olin made a similar observation: "One of the ways you evaluate leaders is if they pick people who are weaker, and then they push you around or if they pick people who are strong and might be good at their own job. And Chuck was unafraid of picking people, the strongest people, and having them around him."

Vest acknowledged how important it was for him to build a strong team of leaders:

> Now in terms of implementation, another thing that I feel very strongly about for a position such as university presidency is that these things can only be done by teams and that the most fundamental thing you have to do is surround yourself with great leaders who complement you.

Vest felt passionately about how important it was for him and his team to promote academic values and support the collegial culture of faculty as a fundamental and uncontestable criterion for selection of his team members.

To further underscore the team dynamics, Vest delegated the oversight of the major projects to his senior leadership team that reflected his academic values. Brown, when he was the dean of engineering, was given the charge of the $300 million Stata Center (along with Sirianni), and later the oversight and coordination of all the academic projects when he became the provost. Bacow was put in charge of overseeing Simmons Hall. Mitchell headed the client team of the Media Lab. Curry oversaw the Brain and Cognitive Sciences building.

Morality

Vest is universally considered to be humble, generous, and respectful. Vest was also known to be a person of integrity who made decisions that were measured, carefully deliberated, resolute, and value-driven. Interviewees corroborated about the "principled" and moral leader who was guided by his conscience.

For instance, commenting extensively about his approach to leadership and management, Vest declared, "Universities are not, and must never become, simply businesses. Our essence and our human purpose run far deeper than that" (Vest, 2005), which hints at leadership that transcends institutional boundaries and operates from a humanistic and moral foundation. Stephen Immerman noted: "The things I remember about Chuck are that he was just and very principled. It didn't matter who you were, and he was respectful of everybody. Even if he disagreed with you, I mean you knew it, but you knew it wasn't about him. I mean ultimately we all have ego, but it really wasn't about him, he truly viewed it as service."

Just as Vest took a moral stance with respect to Krueger's case, the justice department case, and the case of gender equity, he also took moral stances with respect to architectural decisions. His decision-making about architecture was guided by what was right rather than what was the easiest, safest, or the cheapest thing to do. Terman concurred that Vest's decisions were guided by something larger than short term and monetary parameters: "Being a steward of the future is a very complicated thing. That was really Chuck's, the president's role. Stewardship is not always about making the most conservative decision. There are times when you really have to throw yourself into a vision of the future that is maybe more expansive."

Vest felt it was a moral imperative to bring the physical plant in line with the world-class institution that MIT is and the world-class people who make the institution the best in the world. Mitchell characterized Vest's efforts to transform the physical plant as both a moral imperative and a "battle for the soul of MIT" (Mitchell, 2007).

The theme of the "right thing to do" surfaced many times in the interviews and other data, which is a moral argument. Bacow referred to, among other things, Vest's moral stance of "doing the right thing" in making the decisions about architects Gehry and Holl, despite the higher costs they incurred. Furthermore, as many interviewees, including Vest, observed, MIT's physical plant was in serious disrepair at best and dirty, dark, dreary, and unsafe at worst.

Vest, guided by a number of reports and incidents, took it up as a moral responsibility to provide MIT a campus that is people-centered and communal. He valued and created "innovative space" where inspired people actualize their creative potential. Bacow, recalled how "Chuck challenged all of us and said that MIT *should* have a campus that's as creative as the people who occupy it." Vest was guided by the intuition that there needs to be a correspondence, alignment, connection, resonance, and synergy between the people who occupy space, the nature of the space, and the qualities embodied by the architecture of the space, which resulted in a supercharged creative place.

Trustee Ray Stata was unequivocal about Vest's moral leadership: "He always speaks with wisdom. He always speaks in ways that give you trust in his integrity, in his vision and in his judgment."

The pattern of decisions and actions by Vest in a wide array of situations confirm (and confirmed by even his fiercest critics) that he has consistently kept MIT's best interests in mind, and kept his individual tastes and preferences in check. For instance, Vest recalled his conversation with Gehry, where Vest said his personal preference of architectural style would be "red brick Georgian architecture," but that his personal likes and dislikes are not important when it comes to what the institution and a specific situation needs. The incident reveals a principled leader who is disciplined, self-aware, and guided by institutional interests. There is always an inner struggle between consciences to place the collective interests ahead of individual preferences and to resist the compulsion to unilaterally impose one's will over the collective. The presence of struggle and the choice to be guided by conscience, where the higher road is consistently taken, is indicative of a transformative leader and can be found in the case in many instances. Part of Vest's ability to motivate includes his transparency in expressing the inner struggle as well as connecting it with institutional struggles.

Motivation

According to Burns, motivation is the driving force behind transformational leadership. Motivation fosters engagement, builds the team, and inspires the team and other stakeholders to pursue a higher, larger, nobler, respectable and moral purpose that transcends a specific task or project. Motivation is also closely tied to the leader's ability to articulate the purpose, promote shared values, and move beyond the transactions of carrots and sticks. Motivation taps into the followers' inner constitutions. It finds the energy within (transformational) rather than relying on coercion or incentives from the outside (transactional). Further, motivation is not something that results from speeches but from the intrinsic integrity presented tacitly through actions and consistent practices.

John Curry, who enjoyed a successful career in higher education finance and management at the University of Southern California and the California Institute of Technology, was motivated by the excitement and challenge of the scale and character of architectural change at MIT. "The combination of financial modeling and building exciting buildings was too much to keep me in sunny southern California," he said.

Sirianni's motivation was evident when she articulated the common purpose, "audacious innovation." Curry recognized the long-term impact of the Vest era. He compared a pedestrian graduate dormitory building on campus with the more distinctive projects:

> In fifty years nobody will recognize that (run of the mill) building as even remotely related to Massachusetts Institute of Technology. They'll still recognize Saarinen's Chapel, they'll recognize Steven Holl's building, they'll recognize Frank Gehry's building, they'll recognize Alvar Aalto's building, and the list goes on. And they will say that that was particularly MIT.

Bacow observed that Vest "had a way of inspiring people and laying out broad brushstrokes of what he wanted to do." To sum up, as Bacow noted, Vest motivated his team by encouraging them to be creative and thing big. "Chuck encouraged us to dream about how to make MIT a better place. Bill Mitchell, Bob Brown, John Curry, Vicky Sirianni, I mean I could go down the list, other deans, who were all dreaming. . . . It lifted everybody's expectations." As Burns pointed out, motivation is the driving force for transformational leaders to accomplish change. Maslow's theory of motivation is confirmed by Vest's case where motivation resulted from Vest's ability to address the deepest needs of his team members and stakeholders and tap into the highest levels of their hierarchy of needs, approaching self-actualization.

Self-Actualization and 'Making Conscious what Lies Unconscious'

Self-actualization is a notion Burns draws from Abraham Maslow's hierarchy of needs. Individuals or organizations can be said to be self-actualized when they rise above the "lower" needs in Maslow's hierarchy, such as physiological and safety needs, and move beyond the need for self-esteem. The institutional need for self-esteem is often manifested in the desire to move up the rankings, aggressive branding, and developing pride. Self-actualization, on the other hand, is manifested in the realization that the need for self-esteem has already been met, and that the individual or institution needs to spring from a platform of confidence to reach out to engage the world and its problems and opportunities to fully realize its potential. This is what MIT attained during Vest's tenure.

Vest's leadership exemplifies, as discussed so far, a leader who was self-aware, was comfortable selecting individuals who have complementary strengths, and could distinguish between his personal preferences and institutional needs in terms of the kind of architecture the institution needs.

Vest not only moved toward self-actualization himself at MIT, but he also recognized the needs of his team members to fulfill their own potential. His leadership moved the entire team closer to self-actualization, the pinnacle of Maslow's hierarchy of needs.

One of the fundamental concepts behind Maslow's theory of motivation is the notion that motivation is not given from outside but found within the individual when the individual gains a deep understanding of his or her constitution, psychological makeup, and drives and finds a supportive environment in which to explore creativity. Psychoanalytic approaches to leadership, of which Burns's theories are a part, show that transformational leaders are effective in listening, observing, and understanding the followers' psychological needs and help sublimate those needs by guiding team members to highest levels of morality and motivation where the inner challenges and struggles find a positive and affirmative outlet.

Part of the self-actualization process is—for the individual or an institution—Burns said, to "become aware or conscious of what they feel—to feel their true needs so strongly, to define their values so meaningfully, that they can be moved to purposeful action."

While engagement and team building are processes, self-actualization is an end that defines the leader-follower relationship. However, self-actualization could embrace not only the immediate leadership team, but also the architects involved and even the workers who built the projects. To restate what was said in an earlier chapter, the Stata Center did much to excite the stakeholders (or rile the opponents), motivate them (or enrage them), energize them, and provide tangible evidence that MIT was entering a new millennium with new energy. The project allowed architect Frank Gehry to apply his creative and technological ingenuity to engage MIT and thus actualize the potential of both. The project allowed the client team, headed by Robert Brown and Chris Terman, to learn immensely about architectural processes and the larger purposes of architecture and to actualize their potential.

Further, the story of construction workers who left work elsewhere to work on the Stata Center reinforces how Vest's leadership and Gehry's architecture inspired them and helped them realize their potential.

Bacow provided another poignant example when he noted that five of Vest's immediate leadership team went on to become presidents of major research universities, evidence that they actualized their potential.

Taking the analysis to the institutional level, the question becomes, did MIT attain self-actualization through its architecture? Did the institute become what it should have always been?

When Vest arrived at MIT, he began to feel the institute (more on this topic in the next section on Feeling MIT), its burdens, its disheveled physical plant. As Terman expressed it, MIT was "in bed with the government, and that's what paid for a lot of the campus," which resembled, in Vest's words, "a naval base more than a campus for such a wonderful academic community." MIT was crying out to him for a need to not only shift to more diverse revenue streams but also to move to a more academic and institutional ambiance fit for all people, not just a gritty and tough place for grown men to operate machinery. Vest helped address this deep-seated need for the institution to actualize its evolving self.

Further, major parts of MIT, such as the computer science department, were strewn all over the place and housed in rented space at the outskirts of the campus, to the great inconvenience of one-third of MIT's undergrads who majored in computer science at the time. As many interviewees pointed out, MIT's computer science and artificial intelligence units are the premier fountainheads of knowledge in their respective disciplines and deserved prominence and centrality. Vest understood these impulses within the institution and resolved them through the amalgamation of activities in one space in the Stata Center and right across from another vibrant and emerging discipline of neuroscience in the Brain and Cognitive Sciences building.

Architecture, for Vest, became the organizational means through which these latent and strong institutional drives could be fulfilled not just at a physical level but also at emotional and unconscious levels.

Building 20 (the Rad Lab), which was the temporary building originally intended to last just three years, but famously lasted for fifty, played a big role in the psychological makeup of the institute. Not only did remarkable inventions come out of the building, but it also became the beehive of thousands of memories of the people who passed through it. When it could no longer be safely inhabited, it was demolished, opening up space for the Stata Center. In orchestrating this, Vest emblematically, physically, and emotionally swapped spatial paradigms (rundown equipment space with normative and humanized space). More about the aesthetic dimensions of self-actualization will be discussed in the next section, but it suffices to say that a number of voices that remained latent or repressed or ignored prior to Vest's arrival (including those pleading for gender equity or crying out for improved residential life), found a vent through Vest's leadership. In Maslow's terms, the creation of the Stata Center allowed MIT to rise above the lower needs of physiological, safety, and belonging to operate at a higher level of self-actualized artistic plane through Gehry's work.

Burns' framework of transformational leadership alludes to the notion of *conflict* being essential to the process of making *conscious what lies unconscious* in the followers. Burns pointed out the condition of "disagreement over goals within an array of followers, fear of outsiders, competition for scarce resources—immensely invigorates the mobilization of consensus and dissensus" to be a part of the process of self-actualization (Burns, 1978).

One example of how the "unconscious" of the institution was manifested in conflict about architectural choices can be found in the tension that existed between MIT "insiders" who felt threatened by the presence and choices of the "outsiders." The conservatives who had been with the institution for a long time preferred to hire alumni architects already known to MIT. They craved buildings with a fairly consistent image, manageable costs, and predictable results. They trusted that alumni architects understood MIT culture and needs and feared that nonalumni architects would disrupt the *continuity* of patterns of MIT's past.

The role of a leader in bringing unconscious struggles and needs to a conscious plane is to act as the organizational psychoanalyst who at once is involved in the situation and yet is capable of maintaining an outsider perspective. As Burns points out, this may lead to conflicts. Exemplifying the "outsider" role was President Vest—who was relatively new to campus—and others on his team who had been at MIT for different lengths of time but shared Vest's perspective to some degree. The outsiders took a progressive view and saw the opportunities as a historical turning point for the institute. As a challenge to the conservative elements at MIT, Vest, as early as his inauguration time, declared a higher and broader interpretation of MIT's role and position in the world: "To draw boundaries around our institution, to close off the free exchange of education and ideas, would be antithetical to the concept of a great university" (Vest, 2005). In Vest's case, parallels could be seen with Max Weber's notion of the charismatic leader as an outsider (M. Weber & Eisenstadt, 1968).

Vest, in four out of five instances, chose non-MIT graduates as architects for reasons entirely other than the insider-outsider framework. However, for some at MIT, being an MIT graduate was an important criterion for architect selection.

Some critics accused Vest and his team of a "terrible combination of hubris and ignorance," for choosing prominent architects and allowing one project to go over budget. "Moronic nonsense" is how architectural critic Robert Campbell described the choice of Gehry for the Stata Center (Campbell, June 19, 2007). The underlying assumption beneath these accusations is that the *only* reason clients choose prominent architects is to satisfy their own ego, and that any project that runs over budget is due to client's ego and ignorance. The criticism shows that Vest's efforts to make MIT aware of its unconscious had been interpreted in some quarters as irresponsibility.

But, as Mitchell put it, "Mindless commodity architecture should be no more acceptable on college campuses than second-rate physics or banal history." He further said, "it is a fundamental responsibility of universities to pursue architecture and urbanism at the highest intellectual level and the highest level of cultural ambition," (Biemiller, Jan. 28, 2008).

Evidence of MIT's latest attempts at self-actualization could be seen in the institute's first attempts to use architecture to define itself and to actualize itself as appropriate for the times. Vest often remembered the difficulties President Richard Maclaurin had faced nearly a century earlier when he oversaw the development of the present MIT campus. The conservatives of Maclaurin's day worried about architect William Bosworth's "carefree attitude toward cost overruns" and complained that "his beaux-arts background would send him off on artsy tangents." Maclaurin, however, supported Bosworth (Alexander, 2011) and helped MIT reach toward self-actualization in those early days, much as Vest would do decades later.

Transactional Leadership

The key point of this book has been that Vest's case is an example of transformational leadership in higher education. Thus, the key point has been addressed in depth first. Although Burns's account of transformational and transactional leadership is a contrasted one, in reality, the two types of leadership are interrelated. As Burns articulated, transactional leadership is about trading, exchanging, and interacting with others when tasks are accomplished that are economic or political in nature. Most leaders, particularly in the higher education world, operate at the level of transactional leadership (Birnbaum, 1992; Cohen & March, 1986a).

Vest's initial approach to architectural issues was primarily transactional. His strategy stemmed from the recognition—from listening intently to all constituents even before he began his tenure—that the architectural issues needed attention after chronic neglect for nearly a decade by previous administrations. The reconstitution of the building committee after a hiatus of nine years meant the beginning of an institutional process that would advise the president about the physical plant. The committee played a major role all through the campus transformation. The nine-year hiatus also reveals the breakdown of transactional physical plant processes at MIT leading up to Vest's presidency.

The formation of the MIT Task Force on Student Life and Learning, whose recommendations led to the conception of Simmons Hall, could also be seen as a transactional move by Vest. While the issue of gender inequity might initially appear unrelated to architecture, as described in the case, the issue had an impact on humanizing the campus, providing for women and children through spatial accommodation, softening the hardscape, and infusing more humanistic characteristics into campus amenities and facilities in a subtle but significant way. It shifted MIT's identity as a gray factory for men and equipment to that of a place for men and women and mission-driven aesthetic experiences.

Vest respected and followed institutional structures of governance faithfully to the extent that he frequently attended faculty council meetings just to listen to the discussions. That he governed through transparent decision-making has been noted by all the interviewees including those who disagreed with his decisions. Brown, Bacow, Terman, Sirianni, and Immerman have all pointed out how Vest employed a consultative process, listened to all sides, and deliberated matters long enough to arrive at his own conclusions.

Integrating Transformational and Transactional Leadership

In distinction to the notion of transformational leadership, which Burns contrasts with transactional leadership, right from the beginning of Vest's tenure, a pattern of skillfully *combining transactional and transformational approaches* could be seen.

Vest's leadership demonstrates a healthy dynamic between bureaucratic processes of governance (transactional) and principled, executive decision making that stems from moral stances (transformational). While routine decision-making is done all the time with or without leadership intervention, critical decision making invariably involves leadership. How one combines these two aspects is best exemplified by Vest. For instance, the transactional process of the building committee eventually led to a transformational process triggered by a powerful design charrette (intense, short duration collaborative design exercise with unpredictable outcomes) that brought together Pritzker Prize–winning architects to envision the future of the MIT campus (Mitchell, 2007; Simha, 2003).

In summary, Vest's presidency was transformational for MIT, particularly from an aesthetic perspective. Vest led a dynamic and strong leadership team of subordinates. He delegated work to them, inspired them, and cheered when they moved on to become significant academic leaders in their own right. Vest engaged his subordinates at a deep level, elevated them to a higher level of morality, understood the unconscious themes among the stakeholders at the institute and helped make these conscious through his leadership. Team building and moral leadership have been noted to be the strengths of Vest's transformational leadership, based on which he was able to engage, motivate, and help his team and other stakeholders find their verve and actualize their potential.

Vest's case raises questions about the previous assertions by Birnbaum (1992) and Cohen and March (1986) among others who believed that transactional leadership is not only well-suited but also the most desirable form of leadership in academia. Vest's case shows, at least in the context of his leadership at MIT and in science and technology education, that transformational leadership can make a difference. Further, the case hints at potential inconsistencies in Burns's characterization of sharp distinctions between transformational and transactional leadership. The case also questions the polarization present in Zaleznik's framework of leaders and managers. One more lesson to be learned from Vest's example is that not all the elements of transformational leadership (such as engagement, morality, and motivation) are found in equal proportions in every instance; some elements may play a larger role than others. However, Burns's framework does not fully explain the leadership phenomenon in the case of Vest.

The Roads Not Taken

Some challenges Vest and his team faced show how things could have been handled differently throughout the process of feeling, thinking, envisioning, engaging stakeholders, addressing costs, managing risks, communicating the vision, and generally managing the process better.

When there was conflict within Vest's leadership team—which there was—it never amounted to ugliness or viciousness. In fact, as Burns noted, a reasonable amount of conflict is a sign of healthy team dynamics, and the absence of it is indicative of autocratic systems (Burns, 1978a). The highest level of resistance to architectural change came from faculty, alumni, and staff in the *early* stages of the Stata Center process and throughout the Simmons Hall process. In fact, in the later stages of the Stata Center and other academic building projects, there was strong faculty and student support. Just as Vest was shocked by the state of the campus' physical plant when he arrived as the new president at MIT, Gehry's design vignettes shocked the people of MIT with their radically new vision of MIT. Care could have been taken to prototype and vet the public's reaction by testing the aesthetic and communicational adequacy of Gehry's drawings and models before launching a more intentional campaign to present Gehry's ideas for the campus. As noted extensively in the case, critics reacted more to the aesthetic matters than to the functional workings of the Stata Center. Although the highly consultative and engaging design process by Gehry's firm was evidently highly successful in promoting rigorous discussions, feedback from all quarters, countless iterations, and meticulous attention to the larger programmatic issues of function, the early shock appears to have lingered around and persisted even after project completion.

Other questions, though, remain. Why did MIT wait so long to address its physical plant needs? Why did the building committee not meet for nine years prior to the arrival of Vest? The fact that MIT had to build extensively, to the tune of $1 billion, and add enough floor space (*utilitas*) to maintain its competitive edge and deliver on its mission communicates the notion that there were problems in the institutional planning processes. It is not that Vest lavishly spent the money on a spurt of unnecessary buildings and additions and deferred maintenance. On the contrary, MIT needed every bit of space that was added and then more.

Afterword and Conclusions

Presidential leadership in higher education institutions presents a unique challenge as many scholars and practitioners have pointed out (Duderstadt, 2007; Fisher & Koch, 1996a; Kerr, 1984; Lawrence, 2006; L. Weber, Duderstadt, Economica, & James Hosmer Penniman Book Fund, 2004). Examining the case of Charles M. Vest at MIT through a combination of lenses has revealed many lessons about leadership, higher education institutions, and architecture. Transformational leadership matters in colleges and universities. This study revealed that architecture and organizational aesthetics play a larger role in colleges and universities than one might suspect at first glance. As the single largest investment and asset for any institution, the physical plant and architecture encompass all aspects and all stakeholders of an institution, which presents a president with an opportunity—if understood well—to advance the institution's mission and evolve institutional identity through enduring change.

Leaders can benefit from employing the Vitruvian triad of *utilitas*, *firmitas*, and *venustas*; one without the other two could lead to incomplete and inchoate initiatives and actions. Function, structure, and beauty; mission, artifacts, and vision; potential, actual and phenomenal; usability, materiality, and interactivity; efficiency, durability, and sublimity; and thinking, being, and feeling, are ways in which the Vitruvian triad can inform and frame leadership and organizations.

Presidents are uniquely positioned in any organization to employ tacit knowledge and tacit knowing through architecture for sensemaking and strategy-setting. Just as explicit knowledge creation is a central mission for higher education institutions, *tacit knowledge creation* through architecture needs to be recognized as equally crucial for an institution to comprehensively and enduringly deliver on mission. Further, there can be no architectural excellence without the presence and leadership of visionary clients. Architecture owes as much to architects for its advancement as it does to the collaboration of visionary clients (Noever & Rykwert, 2000). Being a good client, for an institution and its presidential team, as Vest's case demonstrated, means that resources serve and follow the mission and identity rather than the other way around.

Identity refers to who one is at present; vision refers to who one wishes to be in the future; and mission refers to one's purpose that drives the vision. Architecture, Vest's case teaches us, is crucial to connect those three dimensions in space and material through well-crafted experiences and provides the president's team and institution with opportunities to excel.

Education, understood from its Latin root *educere*, is *to lead*, a meaning that has been often lost in translation. Just as education is about leadership, leadership is about education, as shown in Vest's leader-making process that led to many university presidencies earned by his former team members. All activities of a higher education institution present opportunities for education, including architecture, its conception, design, development, construction, and inhabitation. The role of place and its architecture will continue to evolve as it has for thousands of years and particularly since the first industrial revolution. As long as aesthetic experiences continue to define humanity at its best (hence we call refined technologies "state of the art"), places that offer beautiful, sublime, tragic, comic, graceful, holy, or other aesthetic experiences will continue to play a role in cultivating human senses and sensibilities as one pursues fulfillment of one's self as a leader, which is the *primary purpose* of education and of architecture in the context of education.

Significance of Vest

Charles Vest's presidency happened at a crucial time for MIT, in the decade leading up to the turn of the millennium. The length of his tenure allowed for a variety of phenomena to bubble up to the surface and people to coalesce. Those fourteen years facilitated long-standing physical plant issues to be addressed in a spurt. As is normally the case with such a growth spurt, the changes happened quickly and became highly visible, marking a major transition point in the institution's history.

Many lessons can be learned from the case of presidential leadership of Vest and his team at MIT. The applicability of the lessons to other contexts could be speculated, and some trajectories of further research could be traced based on the findings. The account of the architectural transformation of the gray factory on the Charles River makes it evident that leadership, organizational aesthetics, and architecture do matter for institutional progress. As the case demonstrated, transformational leaders who understand the power of organizational aesthetics and architecture can make a difference in tangible and lasting ways.

Vest's story demonstrates how a principled leader, with a supportive and collaborative talented team, can use architecture to engage and motivate people by articulating a common purpose, setting the highest expectations of excellence, and influencing the evolution and progress of a higher education institution. Vest made sense of MIT's past and made an effort to resolve institutional incongruities and identity struggles through intentional architectural change. He and his team recognized the mission embodiment potential of architecture and used it effectively to redefine MIT's identity and strategy at the turn of the millennium.

At a time when fiscal pragmatism drives and subtly or overtly subjugates institutional mission and architecture, Vest's story shows it is possible to take a moral stance through and about architecture. It is possible to let institutional identity and vision actually guide architectural decisions. As Winston Churchill said in 1943, "We shape our buildings, and afterwards, they shape us" (Churchill, n.d.). As easy and tempting as it is to let the bottom line drive institutional decisions, Vest's case teaches us afresh that leaders and institutions that display moral fiber, courage, and grace under fire are the ones that come out stronger and prevail in the end owing to their capacity to inspire, motivate, and engage people. Fiscal resources can be raised if an inspiring leader and a compelling cause exist in the first place. As the popular quote attributed to architect and planner Daniel Burnham goes, "Make no little plans; they have no magic to stir men's blood." Vest and his leadership team embodied Burnham's ideal.

The transformational leadership framework by Burns (1978), the Bolman and Deal framework (2008), and any number of other frameworks cited in the literature were silent when it came to aesthetic leadership that is distinguished from symbolic leadership. From Vest's case, it is possible to see that transformational leaders are also aesthetic leaders. In larger social and political arenas of leadership, political leaders such as Mahatma Gandhi, Abraham Lincoln, and Mao Tse-tung were transformational, but they also shared the underlying aesthetic tenor. Transformational leaders are particularly effective at crafting aesthetic experiences and connecting with stakeholders' visceral feelings. By engaging their followers with a common and higher purpose, and by manifesting change in tangible, visible, audible, sensible forms, transformational leaders become architects of change, for which Vest's case is an example.

In his story, we find a reconfirmation of Burns's notion that transformational leadership operates—in Abraham Maslow's hierarchy of needs—at the level of self-actualization, which encompasses morality, creativity, and fulfillment of inner potential (ibid.). Transformational leadership transcends merely setting goals, or marshaling people and resources to achieve those pre-planned goals; instead, it allows for spontaneous emergence of transformative results that can neither be planned nor foreseen. Burns's invocation of self-actualization suggested that creativity and aesthetics are vehicles to bring self-fulfillment.

Vest's leadership involved both transactional and transformational leadership. Depending on the situation, he employed one or the other, or one with the other. The notion that transactional leadership could provide a stable base for transformations is not found in the either-or dialectic of previous literature on transformational leadership (Bensimon, 1989; Birnbaum, 1992; Birnbaum, 2000; Burns, 1978a; Cohen et al., 1972; Cohen & March, 1986a; Zaleznik, 1977; Zaleznik, 1989). It is conceivable and a matter of common experience that transactional leaders could be found everywhere, but those leaders who master transactional leadership and rise to the pinnacles of transformational leadership are rare. Vest's case confirms Selznick's (1957) observation that leadership is not everything and anything that leaders do in high office, but that there are situations and times that call for transformational leadership.

The Importance of the Tacit and the Unconscious

Another dimension of transformational leadership demonstrated by Vest was his ability to sense the unconscious needs, feelings, and struggles of the institution, bring them to the conscious plane, and address them through architecture. Art and architecture have been recognized as connotative, tacit, and figural forms of knowledge associated with the ability to operate on the unconscious (Diamond, 1993; Gosso, 2004; Winer, Anderson, Danze, Institute for Psychoanalysis, & Chicago Psychoanalytic Society, 2006). Vest helped MIT sublimate its creative potential, purge the lingering hegemony of federally funded gray and utilitarian ambiance, and externalize the normative and creative nature of work at the institute through, what Dale and Burrell have called "art-architecture" (Dale & Burrell, 2003). In the case of MIT, the new art-architecture helped and signified the move of the institution away from a federally funded gray factory of equipment space to that of a more creative, humane, and playful campus that extended and reinterpreted the Infinite Corridor as a bustling street in the Stata Center.

Vest intuitively understood and learned from Mitchell the crucial concept that architectural artifacts and spaces are a form of knowledge—*tacit knowledge*—that embodies institutional mission and identity. The conventional image of knowledge is explicit knowledge in the form of textual information compiled in documents that fill cabinets and bookshelves in an office or a library. Things, sounds, smells, and other tacit knowledge are not usually perceived to be knowledge. Epistemologist and philosopher Michael Polanyi (1967) told us otherwise and pointed out that a majority of what we know is not explicit, discursive, linguistic, abstracted, or denotative knowledge. In many disciplines, including architecture, the primary form of knowledge is tacit knowledge in the form of things and buildings that belong to the aesthetic realm, which is experienced through senses and viscerally felt. One of the misconceptions about aesthetics is that some consider them superficial and a luxury, which presents a flawed logic. Consider music, as sound, which is an example of tacit knowledge that activates senses resulting in aesthetic experiences. Good music is not considered a luxury. Good music is not considered a prerogative of the rich and privileged. Good music is certainly not considered to be a premium. People do not ask for mediocre sounds (but they interestingly do ask for mediocre architecture), which might indicate how the sensibility of music is perhaps better cultivated than the sensibility of spatial experiences.

Vest and his team felt that the expectations and criteria of meritocracy and the expectations of excellence at MIT that applies to its faculty members, students, and knowledge creation activities should be extended to the creation of tacit knowledge. To Vest and his team, for a place that treasures its Nobel laureates, Fields medalists, MacArthur "genius" grant winners, national distinguished professors, and other celebrated intellectuals, choosing Pritzker Prize–winning architects felt like a logical decision. However, much of the criticism levied against Vest and his team has been that they chose prominent and celebrated "star" architects.

Vest's case teaches us that architecture should not be reduced to a prosaic mode of real estate development devoid of consideration for aesthetic excellence. The biggest risk a university president can take is, as the case teaches, to divorce architecture from the institution's academic mission and process of education. It is the responsibility of a university president to ensure that architectural knowledge is created in alignment with institutional mission and identity and approached—as one would approach research and teaching—as an academic activity to educate the world. Put differently, a leader could use architecture as a vehicle that could embody what an institution is at present (identity) as well as what the institution wishes to become in the future (vision) and deliver on the mission. At MIT, Vest's decisions were not only consistent with institutional identity but also aspirational about where Vest envisioned the institute should head. In its future-oriented dimension, architecture became a strategic tool for Vest and his team.

Lingering Questions

When I began exploring the case of Charles Vest at MIT, I heard, in architectural circles outside MIT, many voices of dissonance. The voices mentioned "inflated egos, hubris, outrageous costs, and other laughable financial practices," the "extravagance of starchitects," and "complicated buildings that leak and cannot be easily maintained." Some external critics characterized the Stata Center as "ugly" or "strange." Based on such comments, I expected to find people with big egos, gigantic mismanagement, irreconcilable conflicts within the institution, dire financial problems at MIT, and really unhappy users of the new buildings. Instead, I found a case that merits detailed study and possible emulation. While it is true that the Stata Center had leaked and needed to be fixed—which is akin to bug fixing in a software release—complex buildings, ranging from the works of Le Corbusier to Frank Lloyd Wright, had faced leaks when they were first built but are now cherished works of collective cultural heritage.

Vest and his leadership team were well-respected, considered to be humble yet full of integrity, strength, and solid determination to see the projects through. These traits are necessary for the execution of challenging, large-scale, and innovative projects.

Questions do remain about the opportunity cost of investment that went into the campus architecture. Might some of that money been spent on better delivery of the institutional mission? Such a question is difficult to answer as architecture lasts for hundreds of years, serving the institution in myriad ways, and cannot be easily compared with initiatives whose impact lasts a few years or decades.

Implications for Presidents and Leadership Teams

Literature on higher education leadership, particularly presidential leadership, has long touted the desirability of transactional leadership to the exclusion of recognizing the importance of transformational leadership (Birnbaum, 1992; Cohen & March, 1986a). Vest's case shows that transformational leadership is not only possible, but at MIT it made all the difference. The case confirms the elements of Burns's framework of transformational and transactional leadership, but it also shows that the two types of leadership are not mutually exclusive; on the contrary, Vest's case demonstrates how transactional leadership is an essential foundation for transformational leadership.

Debunking the notion that transformational leadership is about personal magnetism or aggressive, abrasive, or ungracious behaviors, and confirming Burns's observations and studies of prominent exemplars from political science, Vest's leadership showed how a sublime, humble, self-effacing personality coupled with the ability to listen deeply to the constituents can lead to a significant change that an institution needs rather than change that a leader demands without consultation. In fact, the elements of Burns's framework of leadership, as Vest demonstrated, show that leaders care deeply about their stakeholders and leadership teams by rising above quotidian transactions and staying focused on a higher, larger, greater, and inspiring common purpose that transcends silo-thinking and inspires followers.

The Vitruvian triad provides a helpful framework for practice for leaders and leadership teams. By using the rubric of three dimensions of leadership—*utilitas, firmitas,* and *venustas*—a leader can aim for balance and engage cognitive as well as aesthetic tools for not only effective, but also elegant, leadership, an experience approaching leadership nirvana.

By understanding the tendencies of normative organizations to move toward utilitarian identity, such as universities becoming more commercial, higher education leaders can avoid moving their institutions away from their normative identities. Identity-driven aesthetic decision-making is essential to organizational change and pursuing a vision of the future. Vision is an aesthetic term.

Forming a senior leadership team is perhaps the most important aspect of a president's job, about which much has been written. A leadership team needs complementary skills, experiences, abilities, personalities, and points of view that not only bring specific subject matter expertise but the ability to balance academic and aesthetic interests with fiscal responsibilities.

One of the challenges posed by architecture to presidents, a majority of whom are educated in areas other than architecture, is to find counsel to not just understand the pragmatics of space needs and financial modeling (expertise for which is relatively abundant), but, even more important, to understand the deeper aesthetic issues and advocacy from the academic community of faculty and students (which is tough to find).

At MIT, Vest's insistence that his team genuinely respects the faculty and advocates on their behalf was what eventually led to the kind of choices he made. When it came to putting people in charge of major projects, Vest chose from the academic ranks—much to the chagrin of some staff members. Choosing the team that complements rather than mirrors a president's capabilities, and putting an absolute premium on integrity above talent, were hallmarks of Vest's vetting of his team members. By doing so, Vest delegated carefully and avoided micromanaging his team or the architects while he made only the high-level decisions.

Implications for Architects and Schools of Architecture

Architects are in a unique position as interpreters of culture (Verganti, 2009). With an ability to mediate between the tacit and explicit knowledge of the built environment, architects bring valuable skill sets and professional expertise. Vest's case illustrates the importance of a close correspondence between an institution's current identity, vision (future identity), and how these two come together through architecture to deliver on the mission. One crucial point that is usually not common knowledge to architects, however, is the *academic nature of the tacit knowledge* they create for higher education institutions. The lesson from Vest's case in this regard is that architects working in an institutional context can don the robes of an academic, take on the triadic mission of an institution—teaching, knowledge creation, and service—and make their work integral to the academic work of the institution by advancing and creating new knowledge. Architecture of an institution—its conception, design, development, and construction—provides opportunities to educate students, faculty, staff, and other stakeholders. Engagement of the MIT School of Architecture and Planning throughout the process and the willingness to take reasonable risks to put educational goals ahead of business goals ultimately yielded dividends for all at MIT. It is perhaps not a coincidence that five out of six primary designers engaged by Vest had extensive teaching experience.

Schools of architecture, if they exist on campus, and their leaders become special resources for presidents who value academic values and are committed to collegial cultures (Bergquist & Pawlak, 2008). Vest's relationship to Dean Mitchell shows the importance of architectural counsel to promote the excellence of architecture at its artistic best. The example shows that, as repositories of architectural knowledge, schools of architecture can be a resource for presidents, and presidents can be well-served to acknowledge and respect the expertise of their own schools, faculty, students, and deans not only for the utilitarian purpose of obtaining advice, but for the symbolic purpose of showing the value and importance of this key resource in collegial cultures (Bergquist & Pawlak, 2008). The architecture of a campus can be leveraged as both a curricular and a co-curricular opportunity and provide lessons in leadership.

Implications for Trustees

Of the myriad criteria trustees use to select a president, aesthetic knowledge is not one of them. Research shows that leaders with creative sensibilities are more effective and more likely to be transformational (Morral, 2012). Selection of a president—an authentic leader who is capable of listening and rallying people with a higher, larger, nobler, and transcending purpose—is the trustees' foremost responsibility. Technical and financial skills could be found in a leadership team, but the inspirational role cannot be tasked out. Vest was chosen for his ability to listen and foster consensus, ability to articulate a higher vision that inspired people, and for his "personable engineer" personality, which ultimately proved to be instrumental in raising over a billion dollars in support of architecture and other initiatives.

In some cases, trustees take an unduly active role on building committees to the exclusion of presidents, deans, and others and engage in micromanagement that results in a dysfunctional situation, which was the case at the University of Texas at Austin (University of Texas at Austin, 1999). As the findings of this study suggest, just as curriculum development or other academic matters are prerogatives of faculty and the president, decisions involving the tacit knowledge creation through architecture should also be considered academic matters. High-level aesthetic decisions—such as choice of architects or aesthetic criteria—are part of a president's prerogative in his or her role as sensemaker, educator-in-chief, and visionary. At MIT, the financial and moral support Vest enjoyed from his trustees such as Ray Stata, Alexander Dreyfoos, Al and Barrie Zesiger, and Richard Simmons was essential to the successful execution of architectural projects. Although they, at times, challenged Vest about the premium he was willing to pay for academic and aesthetic choices, they did not resort to obstructionism, a lesson that becomes an exemplar for boards. It is for this precise reason that the MIT trustees, despite some conservative grumblings, ultimately rose to the occasion and put their resource-raising efforts where they mattered most for the institution, and, following the principle of "keep the noses in and hands out," largely stayed out of the selection of architects and the processes of designing and building the projects.

Suggestions for Further Research

Five topics that directly relate to the theoretical lenses used in this book could be explored further with respect to leadership:

1. Transformational leadership in academic institutions
2. Aesthetic leadership and the intersections between transformational and aesthetic leadership
3. Correspondence between tacit and explicit knowledge of an institution and their relationship to mission
4. Leadership and tacit knowledge
5. The future of campus-based education

There is a paucity of leadership studies focused on transformational leadership in academic institutions, as noted earlier. The prevailing position held by many scholars of academic leadership is to describe college presidency as a transactional job, a position that has been contested by few (Fisher & Koch, 1996a, p. ix). Most vocal of the transactionalists, Robert Birnbaum was critical of the notions of transformational leadership or charismatic leadership in the academic world (Birnbaum, 1992). He calls the notions of transformational leadership myths and tries to articulate how those notions are either not sensible, non-existent, or too elusive in the context of colleges and universities. Birnbaum equates transformational leadership to frequent, unreasonable, leader-centric actions that threaten the stability and peace of an academic institution, which he mistakes as transformational leadership. Burns does not call autocratic individuals leaders, let alone transformational leaders. The current book puts a dent in Birnbaum's arguments and assumptions. Further studies of transformational leadership might reveal why it is a rarity and could examine the factors that contribute to such a situation rather than assuming that such leadership is not well suited to academic institutions.

Scholarship on aesthetic leadership and organizational aesthetics, and leadership studied through those frameworks, can be traced back only twenty years at best and should be considered an emerging field that needs much interdisciplinary attention. From existing literature, it is clear that the notion of charismatic leadership and transformational leadership are closely related concepts and spring from an aesthetic foundation.

Most studies on leadership examine the utilitarian aspects of leadership (productivity, effectiveness, etc.) and structural aspects of leadership (role in the organization), but not on the aesthetic aspects of leadership. Few studies that do exist show positive relationships between the artistic abilities of leaders and their effectiveness. Given that most college and university presidents have backgrounds in education, humanities, or social sciences, it is crucial to understand the aesthetic dimensions of leadership and, as an extension, of organizations.

Related to aesthetics is the notion of tacit knowledge (Polanyi, 1967). The notion is foundational to Donald Schön's work (Schön, 1999) that informs ways of understanding and approaching leadership that expose the limitations of cognitive, rational models of leadership.

Art and architecture are fundamentally connotative as opposed to denotative, figural as opposed to discursive, and tacit as opposed to explicit. Leadership as practice consists largely of tacit learning and knowing. Tacit knowledge informs leadership in at least two ways. First, it informs leadership as practice. Second, it reveals how organizations are manifestations of large amounts of tacit knowledge such as architecture and arts. There is much to be understood about the importance of tacit knowledge with respect to leadership in general and in the context of academic institutions in particular. This book furthers the scholarship about the tacit dimensions of leadership but suggests great potential for further study that explores how leaders learn and practice through tacit learning and how institutions embody tacit knowledge in their physical environments.

Another topic that merits further study is about the role of a physical plant at a time when technology is reshaping community and the sense of place. In what ways does the role of a physical plant change, if any? In what ways does the physical plant become essential or marginal to learning? What will campus mean in the age of networked learning technologies and related pedagogical methods? Extending the exposition by Bergquist and Pawlak about "tangible cultures" in academia, how central or marginal do such cultures that are centered on architecture become in facilitating tacit or explicit learning? Are institutions changing the level of commitment to their physical plants as we enter a more intensely global and networked world? How can leaders in higher education understand and lead architectural changes that typically are the single largest investment for an institution?

Finally, it is important to further study the applicability and relevance of transformational leadership and organizational aesthetics in the heterogeneous field of higher education, a world that consists of institutions of all sizes, sectors, and types. I hope this book not only fills some gaps in literature or raises new questions but also leads to further studies that advance the worlds of architecture, leadership, and higher education.

Appendix A: Timeline of Key Events at MIT

Table 7.1.   Appendix A: Timeline of Key Events at MIT

1861	MIT founded by William Barton Rogers
1913	MITs purchases the Cambridge site
1916	MIT's new campus designed by William Welles Bosworth opens under President Richard Maclaurin's leadership
1946	Baker House residence hall designed by Finnish architect Alvar Aalto opens
1955	MIT Chapel designed by Eero Saarinen opens
1956	Kresge Auditorium designed by Eero Saarinen opens
1988	Building 20 (Radiation Laboratory) slated for eventual demolition
Oct. 15, 1990	President Chuck Vest joins MIT
May 10, 1991	President Vest inaugurated as the fifthteenth president of MIT
May 22, 1991	U.S. Department of Justice sues MIT and eight members of Ivy League universities for alleged violation of Sherman Antitrust Act. All Ivy League universities sign a consent decree with the justice department, but MIT goes to trial.
August, 1991	MIT opens a Washington, D.C., office
1992	William Mitchell appointed dean of School of Architecture and Planning and architectural advisor to the president MIT concludes "The Campaign for the Future," raising $700 million
July 1, 1993	Victoria Sirianni, a longtime member of physical plant, appointed as the director of physical plant
September 1992	MIT loses the U.S. Department of Justice lawsuit in district court
September 1993	MIT wins the U.S. Department of Justice lawsuit in appeals court
June 1995	Joel Moses appointed provost, succeeding Mark Wrighton
January 15, 1996	Robert Brown appointed dean of the School of Engineering
Sept. 29, 1997	Student Scott Krueger of Phi Gamma Delta fraternity dies from alcohol poisoning
1997–1998	Frank Gehry selected as architect for Ray and Maria Stata Center. Alexander Dreyfoos and William H. Gates pledge money for the building that replaces Building 20
March 1998	Building 20 demolished
August 1998	Lawrence Bacow appointed third chancellor Robert Brown appointed provost President Vest announces moving all freshman into on-campus housing by 2001
Nov 15, 1998	William Dickson retires as senior vice president (facilities) after forty years of service John Curry appointed executive vice president

1999	Study on the status of women faculty
March 1999	Bill Mitchell conducts a design forum involving architects Charles Correa, Harry Ellenzweig, Frank O. Gehry, Steven Holl, Fumihiko Maki, and Laurie Olin in discussion of future direction for campus development
November 1999	Vest announces $1.5 billion campaign
Fall 2000	MIT settles for $6 million in Scott Krueger's death
2000	McGovern Institute for Brain Research established
2001	MIT announces OpenCourseWare
Oct 4, 2002	Zesiger Sports and Fitness Center, designed by Kevin Roche, opens Simmons Hall, designed by Steven Holl, opens
2003	Laboratory for Computer Science merges with Artificial Intelligence Laboratory to form CSAIL
May 5, 2004	Stata Center dedication ceremony
Dec. 6, 2004	President Vest leaves office
Dec. 2, 2005	Brain and Cognitive Sciences Complex dedication ceremony
March 5, 2010	Media Laboratory building opens
Dec. 12, 2013	Charles Vest passes away in Washington D.C. area after a battle with pancreatic cancer

Appendix B: Research Design and Methods

As this study intends to understand a complex phenomenon with multiple variables and issues that require further understanding, a qualitative approach was chosen. Specifically, the case study method has been identified due to the explanatory and descriptive nature of the study. Case study method is characterized by the need for multiple kinds and sources of data, and multiple perspectives are needed to analyze the data. The unit of analysis in this study is the leader, but the context for the study encompasses other organizational actors, decisions, motives, and architectural constructs. Consistent with the case study method, I served as the instrument of primary data collection and interpretive analysis.

The study examines presidential leadership that transformed the architecture of an institution at the scale of the campus. A pilot study was conducted in February through April 2012 to identity potential cases, evaluate feasibility, and gather preliminary data to demonstrate viability. The pilot study examined many potential cases and tested them against the following selection criteria based on the framework of transformational change developed by Eckel, Hill, and Green (1998, p. 3):

1. Change alters the culture of the institution; (2) Change is deep and pervasive, affecting the whole institution; (3) Change is intentional; and (4) Change occurs over time.

Based on this rubric, the following detailed criteria—that corresponded to the Eckel, Hill, and Green's rubric—were developed for site selection:

1. Significant level of resources must have been committed to demonstrate the level of commitment exercised by the president. $1 billion emerged as a threshold from the study of potential cases in the pilot study.
2. Campus physical transformation initiated by and substantially completed under the tenure of a single president, with evidence of intentional aesthetic choices exercised by the president (such as choosing a particular architect for a project for aesthetic reasons).
3. Organizational identity and questions about mission implicated and indicated by the amount of discussion or controversy generated among stakeholders about the appropriateness of architecture

in the context of what an institution is (identity) and what an institution does (mission) and what an institution wants to be (vision).

One of the findings of the pilot study was that it is interestingly and exceedingly rare to find intentional architectural change at the scale of the campus that directly involves presidential leadership. A number of organizations—such as Society for College and University Planning and Association of University Architects—and individuals at different higher education institutions known for architectural change were approached to identify potential cases. At the end of the pilot study, Vest's presidency was selected as the *only* case that met the selection criteria. Thus, after a rigorous evaluation of the study goals and available cases, it was decided to conduct a single-site case study of Vest's leadership of architectural change at the Massachusetts Institute of Technology.

Data Collection

The following data were collected:

1. **Interviews** (primary data)
   a. President Charles Vest
   b. **Former members** of Vest's leadership team between 1990 and 2004, and a member of the campus master planning team.
2. **Existing scholarly sources** such as books and refereed articles about Vest related to the changes he led at the institution.
3. **Reports to the president** (1871–present). Reports from all corners of the institute to the president reveal different facets of institutional dialogue. Records from around 1990–2004 were examined.
4. **MIT faculty reports** archive (1949–present). From time to time, MIT presidents called on faculty through ad hoc and standing committees. The topics included student life, campus race and diversity issues, and university planning. Reports relevant to Vest's presidency were studied.
5. **MIT Student Life and Learning Task Force** reports and Web-based discussion groups. The collection contains important information about the events in the early 1990s that brought about changes to campus housing.
6. **MIT Presidents'** archive, Charles Vest years 1990–2004.
   a. List of speeches and interviews by Vest
   b. Presidential papers
   c. Annual reports of the president
7. **MIT Oral Histories** archive online:

   a. Interviews of William Dickson, director-emeritus of physical plant and then-senior vice president

8. **MIT faculty newsletter** archives contain candid and spontaneous commentaries, letters, and interviews that reflected the issues of the day. A preliminary search turned up much pertinent material that sheds light on Vest's presidency and the issues of organizational aesthetics and identity.

9. **MIT news office archives** contain voluminous data on a range of topics.

The number of projects undertaken and completed under Vest's tenure was large and involved new buildings, renovations, landscape design, and other physical plant upgrades. For the purpose of the study, two new projects were chosen: An academic facility, the Ray and Maria Stata Center, and a 350-bed dormitory, Simmons Hall. Data pointed repeatedly to the pivotal and iconic nature of these two projects. Many interviewees cited these two projects as emblematic projects for MIT's new direction at the turn of the millennium. The projects were lightning rods for criticism on many fronts and were designed by prominent architects, Frank Gehry and Steven Holl respectively.

References

Abel, C. (1981). Function of tacit knowing in learning to design. *Design Studies, 2*(4), 209–214.

Albert, S., and Whetten, D. A. (2004). Organizational identity. In M. J. Hatch and M. Schultz (Eds.), *Organizational identity: A reader* (pp. 89–118). Oxford, UK: Oxford University Press.

Alexander, P. N. (2011). *A widening sphere: Evolving cultures at MIT.* Cambridge, MA: MIT Press.

Alvesson, M., and Berg, P. O. (1992). *Corporate culture and organizational symbolism: An overview.* Berlin: De Gruyter.

Ancona, D. (2012). Sensemaking: Framing and acting in the unknown. In S. A. Snook, N. Nohria, and R. Khurana (Eds.), *The handbook for teaching leadership: Knowing, doing, and being* (pp. 3–20). Thousand Oaks, CA: Sage.

Antonakis, J. (2012). Transformational and charismatic leadership. In D. V. Day and J. Antonakis (Eds.), *The nature of leadership* (2nd ed., pp. 256–288). Thousand Oaks, CA: Sage.

Arum, R., and Roksa, J. (2010). *Academically adrift: Limited learning on college campuses.* Chicago, IL: University of Chicago Press.

Bass, B. M. (1985a). *Leadership and performance beyond expectations.* New York: Free Press.

Bass, B. M. (1985b). *Leadership and performance beyond expectations.* New York: Free Press.

Bass, B. M. (1990). From transactional to transformational leadership: Learning to share the vision *Organizational Dynamics, 18*(3), 19–31. doi:10.1016/0090-2616(90)90061-S

Bass, B. M., Stogdill, R. M., and Stogdill, R. M. (1990). *Bass & Stogdill's handbook of leadership: Theory, research, and managerial applications* (3rd ed.). New York; London: Free Press; Collier Macmillan.

Bennis, W. G. (1994). *An invented life: Reflections on leadership and change.* New York, NY: Basic Books.

Bennis, W. G., and Nanus, B. (1997). *Leaders: Strategies for taking charge.* New York, NY: Harper Business.

Bensimon, E. M. (1989). In Neumann A., Birnbaum R. (Eds.), *Making sense of administrative leadership: The "L" word in higher education.* School of Education and Human Development George Washington University: Washington, D.C.

Bergquist, W. H., and Pawlak, K. (2008). *Engaging the six cultures of the academy: Revised and expanded edition of the four cultures of the academy.* San Francisco, CA: Jossey-Bass.

Berlin, J. (1990). New MIT president lauded. Retrieved 1/19/2013 from http://www.thecrimson.com/article/1990/6/25/new-mit-president-lauded-palthough-mits/.

Biemiller, L. (Jan. 28, 2008). At Yale, architects consider universities as patrons—buildings and grounds. Retrieved fromhttp://chronicle.com/blogs/buildings/at-yale-architects-consider-universities-as-patrons/4971.

Birks, T., and Holford, M. (1972). *Building the new universities.* Newton Abbot, UK: David and Charles.

Birnbaum, R. (1988). *How colleges work: The cybernetics of academic organization and leadership* (1st ed.). San Francisco, CA: Jossey-Bass.

Birnbaum, R. (1992). *How academic leadership works: Understanding success and failure in the college presidency* (1st ed.). San Francisco: Jossey-Bass.

154   *References*

Birnbaum, R. (2000). *Management fads in higher education: Where they come from, what they do, why they fail*. San Francisco, CA: Jossey-Bass.

Bittner, M. (1986). *West Greenlandic* by Michael Fortescue, Review. *Language in Society*, 15(2), 269–273.

Bok, D. C. (2006). *Our underachieving colleges: A candid look at how much students learn and why they should be learning more*. Princeton: Princeton University Press.

Bolman, L. G., and Deal, T. E. (2008). *Reframing organizations: Artistry, choice, and leadership* (4th ed.). San Francisco, CA: Jossey-Bass.

Boston's big dig gets bigger. (2001, Jan 2001). *Building Design & Construction, 42*, 88, 69.

Bousquet, M., (2008). *How the university works higher education and the low-wage nation*. New York, NY: New York University Press.

Bowen, W. G. (2011). *Lessons learned: Reflections of a university president*. Princeton, N.J.: Princeton University Press.

Boyer, E. L. (1994). Creating the new American college. *Chronicle of Higher Education, 9*, A48.

Broadbent, G., Bunt, R., and Jencks, C. (1980). *Signs, symbols, and architecture*. Hoboken, NJ: Wiley.

Brodie, H. K. H., and Banner, L. (2005). *The research university presidency in the late twentieth century: A life Cycle/Case history approach*. Westport, CT: Praeger Publishers.

Brown, D. G. (2006). *University presidents as moral leaders*. Westport, CT: Praeger.

Bryant F. Tolles, J. (2011). *Architecture & academe: College buildings in New England before 1860*. Lebanon, NH: University Press of New England.

Bullock, N., Dickens, P., and Steadman, P. (1968). *A theoretical basis for university planning*. Land Use and Built Form Studies: Cambridge University School of Architecture.

Burns, J. M. (1978a). *Leadership*. New York, NY: Harper & Row.

Burns, J. M. (1978b). *Leadership* (1st ed.). New York, NY: Harper & Row.

Calvino, I. (1974). *Invisible cities*. New York, NY: Harcourt Brace Jovanovich.

Campbell, R. (June 19, 2007). Does Gehry's Stata center really work? Retrieved 12/28/2012, from http://www.businessweek.com/stories/2007-06-19/does-gehrys-stata-center-really-work-businessweek-business-news-stock-market-and-financial-advice.

Chaffee, E. E., and Tierney, W. G. (1988). *Collegiate culture and leadership strategies*. New York: Macmillan Pub. Co.

Chamberlain, L. (2004). MIT v. Holl. Retrieved 1/8/2013, from http://www.metropolismag.com/story/20040501/mit-v-holl.

Chapman, P. (2006). *American places: In search of the twenty-first century campus*. Santa Barbara, CA: Praeger Publishers.

Christensen, C. M. (2005). *The innovator's dilemma: The revolutionary book that will change the way you do business*. New York, NY: Collins Business Essentials.

Christensen, C. M., and Eyring, H. J. (2011). *The innovative university: Changing the DNA of higher education from the inside out* (1st ed.). San Francisco, CA: Jossey-Bass.

Christensen, C. M., Horn, M. B., and Johnson, C. W. (2008). *Disrupting class: How disruptive innovation will change the way the world learns*. New York, NY: McGraw-Hill.

Churchill, W. (n.d.). Famous quotations and stories Retrieved 3/22/2013, from http://www.winstonchurchill.org/learn/speeches/quotations.

Cohan, P. (2013). How MIT's Kendall Square attracted $2 billion and so can you. Retrieved 1/6/2013, from http://www.forbes.com/sites/petercohan/2013/01/02/how-mits-kendall-square-attracted-2-billion-and-so-can-you/.

Cohen, M. D., and March, J. G. (1986a). *Leadership and ambiguity: The American college president*. Boston, MA: Harvard Business School Press.

Cohen, M. D., and March, J. G. (1986b). *Leadership and ambiguity: The American college president*. Boston, MA: Harvard Business School Press.

Cohen, M. D., March, J. G., and Olsen, J. P. (1972). A garbage can model of organizational choice. *Administrative Science Quarterly, 17*(1), pp. 1–25.

Coulson, J., Roberts, P., and Taylor, I. (2010). *University planning and architecture: The search for perfection.* New York, NY: Routledge.

Creswell, J. W. (2007). *Qualitative inquiry and research design: Choosing among five approaches.* Thousand Oaks, CA: Sage Publications.

Dale, K., and Burrell, G. (2003). An-aesthetics and architecture. *Art and aesthetics at work* (pp. 155–173). Basingstoke, NY: Palgrave Macmillan.

Danısman, A. (2010). Good intentions and failed implementations: Understanding culture-based resistance to organizational change. *European Journal of Work & Organizational Psychology, 19*(2), 200–220. doi:10.1080/13594320902850541

Day, D. V., and Antonakis, J. (2011). *The nature of leadership.* Thousand Oaks, CA: Sage.

Deckstein, D. (March 30, 2011). Jumbo problems: Dreamliner becomes a nightmare for Boeing. Retrieved 1/9/2013 from http://www.spiegel.de/international/business/jumbo-problems-dreamliner-becomes-a-nightmare-for-boeing-a-753891.html.

Diamond, M. A. (1993). *The unconscious life of organizations: Interpreting organizational identity.* Westport, CT: Quorum Books.

Diesenhouse, S. (2000, March 5, 2000). Convention center shapes Boston harbor area. *New York Times* (1923–Current File), pp. RE7.

Dober, R. P. (1992). *Campus design.* Hoboken, NJ: John Wiley.

Downton, J. V. (1973). *Rebel leadership: Commitment and charisma in the revolutionary process.* New York: The Free Press.

Duderstadt, J. J. (2007). *The view from the helm: Leading the American university during an era of change.* Ann Arbor, MI: The University of Michigan Press.

Eckel, P. D., and Kezar, A. J. (2003). *Taking the reins: Institutional transformation in higher education.* Westport, CT: Praeger.

Eckel, P., Hill, B., and Green, M. (1998). *En route to transformation. On change: An occasional paper series of the ACE project on leadership and institutional transformation* American Council on Education Fulfillment Services, Department 191, Washington, DC 20055-0191.

Eco, U. (1979). *A theory of semiotics.* Bloomington, IN: Indiana University Press.

Eisenberg, E. M. (2006). Karl Weick and the aesthetics of contingency *Organization Studies, 27*(11), 1693-1707. doi:10.1177/0170840606068348

Elstak, M. N. (2008). The paradox of the organizational identity field. *Corporate Reputation Review, 11*(3), 277–281. doi:10.1057/crr.2008.22

Erikson, E. H. (1964). *Insight and responsibility; lectures on the ethical implications of psychoanalytic insight* (1st ed.). New York: W. W. Norton.

Ferreira, A. I., and Hill, M. M. (2008). Organisational cultures in public and private Portuguese universities: A case study. *Higher Education, 55*(6), pp. 637–650.

Fisher, J. L. (1984). *Power of the presidency.* New York: Macmillan.

Fisher, J. L., and Koch, J. V. (1996a). *Presidential leadership: Making a difference.* Phoenix, AZ: Oryx Press.

Fisher, J. L., and Koch, J. V.,. (1996b). *The presidency.* Phoenix, AZ: Oryx Press.

Fisher, J. L., Tack, M. W., and Wheeler, K. J. (1988). *The effective college president.* New York; London: Macmillan Pub. Co.

Fortescue, M. D. (1984). *West Greenlandic.* London, UK: Croom Helm.

Frank, K. A., and Fahrbach, K. (1999). Organization culture as a complex system: Balance and information in models of influence and selection. *Organization Science, 10* (3, Special Issue: Application of Complexity Theory to Organization Science), pp. 253–277.

Frederic Golden. (1999, Dec 31, 1999). Person of the century: Albert Einstein (1879–1955). *Time, 154*, 62–65.

Fussman, G. (1986). Symbolism of the Buddhist stūpa. *Journal of the International Association of Buddhist Studies, 9*(2), 37–53.

Gagliardi, P. (1990). *Symbols and artifacts: Views of the corporate landscape.* Berlin: De Gruyter.

Gannon, T. (2004). *Steven Holl Architects/Simmons building: Source books in architecture 5.* Princeton, NJ: Princeton Architectural Press.

Giedion, S. (1967). *Space, time and architecture: The growth of a new tradition.* Cambridge, MA: Harvard University Press.

Goho, A. (2003). MIT in Washington, DC - MIT technology review Retrieved 2/8/2013 from http://m.technologyreview.com/news/401865/mit-in-washington-dc/.

Gosso, S. (2004). *Psychoanalysis and art: Kleinian perspectives.* London, UK; New York, NY: Karnac.

Grafton, K. S. (2009). *Presidential transformational leadership practices: Analysis of self-perceptions and observers at community colleges in Oklahoma.* (D.B.A., University of Phoenix). *ProQuest Dissertations and Theses.* (305123213).

Grosso, F. A. (2008). *Motivating faculty through transformational leadership: A study of the relationship between presidential leadership behaviors and faculty behaviors.* (PhD, The Catholic University of America). *ProQuest Dissertations and Theses.* (304666366).

Gunderson, M. (2000, Spring 2000). A flaw in the system: The fight over UT's Blanton museum. *Cite 47 Cite Magazine, 47,* 34.

Gupta, V. (2011). Cultural basis of high performance organizations. *International Journal of Commerce & Management, 21*(3), 221–240. doi:10.1108/10569211111165280

Hancock, P., and Carr, A. N. (2003). Art and aesthetics at work doi:10.1057/9780230554641

Hawkinson, J., McGraw-Herdeg, M., and Nelson, M. (2009). MIT's endowment over the past ten years. Retrieved 3/24/2013 from http://tech.mit.edu/V129/N43/endowment.html.

Head, S. R. (2009). *Turning the Titanic around: A study of presidential leadership at faith-based institutions that have undergone a transformational change.* (EdD, University of Pennsylvania). *ProQuest Dissertations and Theses.* (304982879).

Hempowicz, C. D. (2010). *Transformational leadership characteristics of college and university presidents of private, title III and title V-eligible institutions.* (EdD, University of Bridgeport). *ProQuest Dissertations and Theses.* (878892691).

Hiltzik, M. (2011). 787 Dreamliner teaches Boeing costly lesson on outsourcing. Retrieved 1/9/2013 from http://articles.latimes.com/2011/feb/15/business/la-fi-hiltzik-20110215.

Höpfl, H. J., and Linstead, S. (2000). *The aesthetics of organization.* Thousand Oaks, Calif.; London: SAGE.

Howell, J. M., and Avolio, B. J. (1992). The ethics of charismatic leadership: Submission or liberation? *The Executive, 6*(2), pp. 43–54.

Hughes, T. P. (2008). MIT architecture and values: Gehry's Stata and Holl's Simmons *History and Technology, 24*(3), 207–220. doi:10.1080/07341510801900250

Jencks, C. (1991). *The language of post-modern architecture.* Academy Editions.

Joyce, N., and Gehry, F. O. (2004). *Building Stata: The design and construction of Frank O. Gehry's Stata center at MIT.* Cambridge: MIT Press.

Kaiser, D. (2010). *Becoming MIT: Moments of decision.* Cambridge, MA: MIT Press.

Kamenetz, A. (2006). *Generation debt: Why now is a terrible time to be young.* New York, NY: Riverhead Books/Penguin.

Kant, I., and Meredith, J. C. (1952). *The critique of judgement.* Oxford: Clarendon Press.

Karagianis, L. (2004). Empowering the world. Retrieved 3/5/2013 from http://spectrum.mit.edu/articles/features/empowering-the-world/.

Kenney, D. R., Dumont, R., and Kenney, G. (2005). *Mission and place: Strengthening learning and community through campus design.* Westport, CT: Praeger.

Kerr, C. (1984). *Presidents make a difference: Strengthening leadership in colleges and universities: A report of the commission on strengthening presidential leadership.* Washington, D.C.: AGB.

Kerr, C. (2001). Academic triumphs a personal memoir of the University of California, 1949–1967. Retrieved

Kezar, A. J. (2001). *Understanding and facilitating organizational change in the 21st century: Recent research and conceptualizations.* San Francisco, CA: Jossey-Bass.

Kiley, K. (12/20/2011). Cornell and Technion's win in New York competition reflects desire to grow urban ties | inside higher ed Retrieved 2/21/2012 from http://www.

insidehighered.com/news/2011/12/20/cornell-and-technions-win-new-york-competition-reflects-desire-grow-urban-ties.

Kolac, E. (2010). *University campus design* LAP Lambert Acad. Publ.

Kondakci, Y., and Broeck, H. V. D. (2009). Institutional imperatives versus emergent dynamics: A case study on continuous change in higher education. *Higher Education, 58*(4), pp. 439–464.

Kormondy, E. J., and Keith, K. M. (2008). *Nine university presidents who saved their institutions: The difference in effective administration.* Edwin Mellen Press.

Kuhn, T. S. (1970). *The structure of scientific revolutions* (2d, enl. ed.). Chicago: University of Chicago Press.

Ladkin, D. (2006). The enchantment of the charismatic leader: Charisma reconsidered as aesthetic encounter *Leadership, 2*(2), 165–179. doi:10.1177/1742715006062933

Lawrence, F. L. (2006). *Leadership in higher education: Views from the presidency.* Transaction Pub.

Lazerson, M. (2010). *Higher education and the American dream: Success and its discontents.* Budapest, Hungary; New York, NY: Central European University Press.

Lederman, D. (2011). Perspectives on the downturn: A survey of presidents. Retrieved 11/25/2011 from http://www.insidehighered.com/news/survey/president2011.

Levy, A. and Merry, U. (1986). *Organizational transformation: Approaches, strategies, theories.* New York: Praeger.

Lima, J. D. F. (1969). *General principles of university planning.* Florianopolis.

Lindquist, J. (1978). *Strategies for change.* Berkeley: Pacific Soundings Press.

Loewe, R. D. (1998). *A professional's guide to college planning.* National Underwriter Company.

Lueddeke, G. R. (1999). Toward a constructivist framework for guiding change and innovation in higher education. *The Journal of Higher Education, 70*(3), 235. doi:10.2307/2649196

March, J. G. (1981). Footnotes to organizational change. *Administrative science quarterly,* 563–577.

March, J. G. (2006). Rationality, foolishness, and adaptive intelligence. *Strategic management journal, 27*(3), 201–214.

Martin, J. L. (2001). *Organizational culture: Mapping the terrain.* Thousand Oaks, Calif.; London: Sage.

Massy, W. F. (2003). *Honoring the trust: Quality and cost containment in higher education.* Bolton, MA: Anker Pub.

McEwen, I. K. (2003). *Vitruvius: Writing the body of architecture.* Cambridge, MA: MIT Press.

Meyerson, D., & Martin, J. (1987). Cultural change: An integration of three different views. *Journal of Management Studies, 24*(6), 623–647. doi:10.1111/j.1467-6486.1987.tb00466.x

MIT in popular culture. (n.d.). Retrieved 2/26/2013 from http://libguides.mit.edu/mitpopculture.

MIT Media Lab. (2010). In memory: William J. Mitchell. Retrieved 2/14/2013 from http://www.media.mit.edu/people/remembering-bill-mitchell?page=1.

MIT News Office. (1996). Standard & Poor's upgrades MIT bonds to top rating—triple A. Retrieved 3/24/2013 from http://web.mit.edu/newsoffice/1996/triplea-rating.html.

MIT News Office. (2001). MIT sells $250M in bonds for construction. Retrieved 3/24/2013 from http://web.mit.edu/newsoffice/2001/bonds-0613.html.

MIT News Office. (2005). Vice President Stowe to retire. Retrieved 1/11/2013 from http://web.mit.edu/newsoffice/2005/stowe.html.

Mitchell, W. J. (2007). *Imagining MIT: Designing a campus for the twenty-first century.* Cambridge, MA: MIT Press.

Mitchell, W. J. (1999). MIT reports to the president 1998–1999 / School Of Architecture and Planning Retrieved 3/2/2013 from http://web.mit.edu/annualreports/pres99/10.00.html.

Morgan, G. (2006). *Images of organization.* Thousand Oaks, CA: Sage.

Morral, E. J. (2012). *Transformational leadership and creativity: An in-depth analysis of mediating constructs.* (PhD, University of Nebraska at Omaha). *ProQuest Dissertations and Theses.* (965385340).

Morrill, R. L. (2010). *Strategic leadership: Integrating strategy and leadership in colleges and universities.* Lanham, Md: Rowman & Littlefield.

Nickles, T. (2002). *Thomas Kuhn.* Cambridge, U.K.; New York: Cambridge University Press.

Noever, P., and Rykwert, J. (2000). *Visionary clients for new architecture.* New York, NY: Prestel Pub.

Nohria, N., and Khurana, R. (2010). *Handbook of leadership theory and practice: An HBS centennial colloquium on advancing leadership.* Boston, MA: Harvard Business Press.

Norberg-Schulz, C. (1980). *Genius loci: Towards a phenomenology of architecture* [Genius loci.]. New York: Rizzoli.

Northouse, P. G. (2013). *Leadership: Theory and practice.* Thousand Oaks, CA: Sage.

Padilla, A. (2005). *Portraits in leadership: Six extraordinary university presidents.* Westport, CT: Praeger.

Pearce, M. (2001). *University builders.* Hoboken, NJ: Wiley-Academy.

Pearce, T. (1995). *Leading out loud: The authentic speaker, the credible leader* (1st ed.). San Francisco, CA: Jossey-Bass.

Peterson, T. (2003). *Nightwork: A history of hacks and pranks at MIT.* The MIT Press.

Peterson, T. F. (2011). *Nightwork: A history of hacks and pranks at MIT.* The MIT Press.

Podolny, J., Khurana, R., and Besharov, M. (2010). Revisiting the meaning of leadership. In N. Nohria and R. Khurana (Eds.), *Handbook of leadership theory and practice: An HBS centennial colloquium on advancing leadership* (pp. 65–105). Boston, MA: Harvard Business Press.

Polanyi, M. (1967). *The tacit dimension* (Anchor Books ed.). Garden City, New York: Doubleday & Company, Inc.

Polanyi, M., and Grene, M. G. (1969). *Knowing and being: Essays by Michael Polanyi* University of Chicago Press.

Prator, R. (1963). *The college president.* Washington: Center for Applied Research in Education.

Preziosi, D. (1979). *Architecture, language and meaning: The origins of the built world and its semiotic organization.* Mouton.

Ramaley, J. (2002). Moving mountains: Instituting culture and transformational change. In R. M. Diamond (Ed.), *Field guide to academic leadership* (1st ed., pp. 526). San Francisco, CA: Jossey-Bass.

Rykwert, J. (1982). *The necessity of artifice: Ideas in architecture.* Rizzoli.

Sales, R. (1998). Vest discusses decision on freshman housing. Retrieved 3/24/2013 from http://web.mit.edu/newsoffice/1998/facmeet-0923.html.

Schein, E. H. (1987). *The clinical perspective in fieldwork.* Newbury Park, Calif.: Sage Publications.

Schein, E. H. (1992). *Organizational culture and leadership* (2nd ed.). San Francisco: Jossey-Bass.

Schein, E. H. (1999). *The corporate culture survival guide: Sense and nonsense about culture change* (1st ed.). San Francisco, CA: Jossey-Bass.

Schön, D. A. (1999). *The reflective practitioner.* New York, NY: Basic books.

Schön, D. A. (1995). Knowing-in-action: The new scholarship requires a new epistemology. *Change, 27*(6), 26–34.

Selznick, P. (1957). *Leadership in administration: A sociological interpretation.* New York: Harper & Row.

Sendak, M. (2000). *Three minutes or less: Life lessons from America's greatest writers.* London, UK: Bloomsbury.

Senge, P. M. (1990). *The fifth discipline: The art and practice of the learning organization* (1st ed.). New York, NY: Doubleday.

References

Serifsoy, I. (2012). *The leader's muse: An exploration of how artistic sensibilities inform organizational leadership.* (PhD, Saybrook Graduate School and Research Center). ProQuest Dissertations and Theses. (1019281733).

Silber, J. (2007). *Architecture of the absurd: How "genius" disfigured a practical art.* Quantuck Lane Pr & the Mill rd.

Simha, O. R. (2003). *MIT campus planning, 1960–2000: An annotated chronology.* MIT Press.

Strati, A. (1999). *Organization and aesthetics.* London; Thousand Oaks, CA: Sage.

Strati, A. (2000). The aesthetic approach in organization studies. In S. Linstead and H. Hopfl (eds.), *The aesthetics of organization* (pp. 13–34). London, UK: Sage.

Strati, A. (2010). Aesthetic understanding of work and organizational life: Approaches and research developments. *Sociology Compass, 4*(10), 880–893. doi:10.1111/j.1751-9020.2010.00323.x

Strati, A. (1996). Organizations viewed through the lens of aesthetics. *Organization, 3*(2), 209–218. doi:10.1177/135050849632004

Strauss, J. C. and Curry, J. R. (2002). *Responsibility center management: Lessons from 25 years of decentralized management.* Washington, D.C.: National Association of College and University Business Officers.

Talgam, I. (10/2009). Lead like the great conductors. Retrieved 4/23/2012 from http://www.ted.com/talks/itay_talgam_lead_like_the_great_conductors.html.

Terry, R. W. (1993). *Authentic leadership: Courage in action.* San Francisco: Jossey-Bass Publishers.

Thelin, J. R. (2004). *A history of American higher education.* Baltimore: Johns Hopkins University Press.

Thornton, C. H., and Jaeger, A. J. (2008). The role of culture in institutional and individual approaches to civic responsibility at research universities. *The Journal of Higher Education, 79*(2), pp. 160–182.

Two whole men (editorial). (1955, Sept. 30, 1955). *The Tech,* pp. 2.

University of Texas at Austin. (1999). Lawrence speck resigns as dean of the UT austin school of architecture. Retrieved 2/5/2013 from http://www.utexas.edu/news/1999/11/22/nr_speck/.

Van de Ven, A. H., and Poole, M. S. (1995). Explaining development and change in organizations. *Academy of Management Review, 20*(3), 510.

van Rekom, J., Corley, K., and Ravasi, D. (2008). Extending and advancing theories of organizational identity. *Corporate Reputation Review, 11*(3), 183–188. doi:10.1057/crr.2008.21

Vennochi, J. (2/23/2001). Convention center's over budget? Time to play the blame game. *Boston Globe.*

Verganti, R. (2009). *Design driven innovation: Changing the rules of competition by radically innovating what things mean.* Harvard Business Press.

Vest, C. M. (2005). *Pursuing the endless frontier: Essays on MIT and the role of research universities.* Cambridge, MA: MIT Press.

Vest, C. M. (2007). Afterword. In W. J. Mitchell (Ed.), *Imagining MIT: Designing a campus for the twenty-first century* (p. 142). Cambridge, MA: MIT Press.

Vest, C. M. (Sept. 8, 2000). Letter from MIT President Charles Vest. Retrieved 12/31/2012 from http://web.mit.edu/newsoffice/2000/letter.html.

Vitruvius Pollio and Krohn, F. (1912). *De architectura, libri decem,.* Lipsiae: in aedibus B. G. Teubneri.

Vitruvius Pollio and Morgan, M. H. (1960; 1914). *Vitruvius: The ten books on architecture* [De Architectura.]. New York: Dover Publications.

Walsh, T., and Bowen, W. G. (2011). *Unlocking the gates: How and why leading universities are opening up access to their courses.* Princeton, NJ: Princeton University Press.

Warren, S. (2002). Show me how it feels to work here: Using photography to research organizational aesthetics. Retrieved 4/18/2012 from http://www.ephemeraweb.org/journal/2-3/2-3warren.pdf.

Wasserman, N., Anand, B., and Nohria, N. (2010). When does leadership matter? A contingent opportunities view of CEO leadership. In N. Nohria and R. Khurana (Eds.), *Handbook of leadership theory and practice: An HBS centennial colloquium on advancing leadership.* (pp. 27–64). Boston, MA: Harvard Business Press.

Weber, L., Duderstadt, J. J., Economica, and James Hosmer Penniman Book Fund. (2004). *Reinventing the research university.* London; Paris; Geneva; Washington, DC: Economica; distributed by the Brookings Institution Press.

Weber, M. (1968; 1947). *The theory of social and economic organization.* New York: The Free Press.

Weber, M., and Eisenstadt, S. N. (1968). *Max Weber on charisma and institution building: Selected papers.* Chicago: University of Chicago Press.

Weick, K. E. (1995). *Sensemaking in organizations.* Thousand Oaks, CA: Sage.

Weimer, J. (2008). *Designing and building things: A synthesis of the classical liberal arts and design studies under the concept of the ancient architect vitruvius with applications to the modern college general education program.* (PhD, The Claremont Graduate University). *ProQuest Dissertations and Theses.* (304674144).

Whetten, D. A. (1998). *Identity in organizations: Building theory through conversations.* Thousand Oaks, CA: Sage.

Winer, J. A., Anderson, J. W., and Danze, E., Institute for Psychoanalysis, & Chicago Psychoanalytic Society. (2006). *Psychoanalysis and architecture.* Mental Health Resources.

Wright, S. (2003). Institute tackles budget issues. Retrieved 3/24/2013 from http://web.mit.edu/newsoffice/2003/budget-0924.html.

Wright, S. (Sept. 20, 2000). Face-to-face meeting leads to settlement. Retrieved 12/31/2012 from http://web.mit.edu/newsoffice/2000/settlement-0920.html.

Yukl, G. A. (2011). *Leadership in organizations (8th edition).* Prentice Hall.

Zaleznik, A. (1977). Managers and leaders: Are they different? *Harvard Business Review, 55*(3), 67–78.

Zaleznik, A. (1989). *The managerial mystique: Restoring leadership in business* (1st ed.). New York: Harper & Row.

Zaleznik, A. (1993). *Learning leadership: Cases and commentaries on abuses of power in organizations.* Chicago, Ill.: Bonus Books.

Zami, M. (2010). *Influence of landscape design on the function of university campus.* Lambert Academic Publishing.

Zemsky, R. (2009). *Making reform work: The case for transforming American higher education.* New Brunswick, N.J.: Rutgers University Press.

Zemsky, R., and Finney, J. E. (2010). Changing the subject: Costs, graduation rates, and the importance of re-engineering the undergraduate curriculum. *American Higher Education, 18 / No. 1* (May, 2010), 2/27/2012.

Zumeta, W., Callan, P. M., Breneman, D. W., and Finney, J. E. (2011). *Financing American higher education in an era of global challenge: An agenda for the nation.* Cambridge, MA: Harvard Education Press.

Index

Aalto, Alvar, 61, 97, 98, 114, 116, 146
Abel, Chris, 34
academic institutions: architecture of, 35–36; cultures and leadership challenges in, 49–52; leadership in, 3–4, 135, 136; open and loosely coupled systems in, 23; transformational leadership in, 23–27
aesthetic leadership, 143–144; symbolic leadership differences with, 33, 137
aesthetics, 9, 29, 109; architecture and institutions lenses of, 7–8; beauty and sublimity as, 32–33; categories of, 117; charisma in, 31, 143; experiences in, 2, 3; as foundational element, 2, 3; institutional identity as expression of, 115–116; in leadership, 1–2; misconceptions about, 138–139; mission as expression of, 113–115; multiple words describing, 3; organizational identity closely related to, 43; organizations in, 2–3; Sendak on, 29; sensory experiences of, 3, 29; symbols differ from, 3; as tacit knowledge, 33–35, 113; as topic of philosophical and political discourse, 2; transformational leadership dimension of, 1; Vest fostering shared sense of, 112–113. *See also* organizational aesthetics; venustas
Al and Barrie Zesiger Sports and Fitness Center. *See* Zesiger Sports and Fitness Center
Albert, S., 45, 45–46
alcohol poisoning, 146
Analog Devices, 86
Antonakis, J., 14, 22

Apple, 49, 112
architects, 1; Bacow on selecting, for residence hall, 98–99; case study implications for, 141–142; selection elements of, 86; Vest on, 87–88
De Architectura (Vitruvius), 37
architecture, 1, 42n1, 136, 139; of academic institutions, 35–36; aesthetics and institutions in, 7–8; choices in, 77–79; as embodiment of institutional mission, 5–6; Mitchell on, 131, 138; Strati on corporate, 35; tacit knowledge through, 34, 135; university presidents challenges in, 36
Architecture of the Absurd: How "Genius" Disfigured a Practical Art (Silber), 77
art-architecture, 116, 138
artificial intelligence, 84, 87, 129
Artificial Intelligence Laboratory, 87, 146
Avolio, Bruce, 22

Bacow, Lawrence, 64, 88, 97, 146; as dream team member, 65–66; example of actualized potential, 128; on male population at MIT, 73; on selecting architect for residence hall, 98–99; Simmons Hall building involvement of, 97, 98, 101, 125; on Vest, 66, 70, 123, 124, 126, 127; on Vest as mentor, 69; on Vest's morality, 125
Baker House residence hall, 61, 97, 98, 116, 146
Bass, Bernard, 14, 17
beauty, 32, 117, 117–118; aesthetics as, 32–33; Vest on distinguishing sublime from, 117
Belluschi, Pietro, 64

Western Greenlandic language, 3
West Virginia University, 55, 66
Whetten, D. A., 45, 45–46
women faculty: study on status of,
   72–73, 79, 146; Vest on MIT
   admitting more, 73–74
World Wide Web, 6, 62
Wright, Frank Lloyd, 40, 139
Wrighton, Mark, 146

Young, John, 58
Yukl, Gary, 14, 15, 24

Zaleznik, Abraham, 8, 18, 21, 22, 47,
   133
Zesiger, Al, 142
Zesiger, Barrie, 142
Zesiger Sports and Fitness Center, 74,
   104, 117, 146

About the Author

Mahesh Daas, EdD, DPACSA, is an award-winning designer and serves as the Dean of the School of Architecture, Design & Planning at the University of Kansas, Lawrence. He is an Association of Collegiate Schools of Architecture distinguished professor and a perpetual member of the ACSA's College of Distinguished Professors. Daas holds a master's degree in architecture from Kansas State University and an executive doctorate in higher education management from the Graduate School of Education at the University of Pennsylvania.